Organizational Consultation

THE COUNSELING PSYCHOLOGIST
CASEBOOK SERIES

SERIES EDITOR: BRUCE R. FRETZ
University of Maryland

Sponsored by the Division of Counseling Psychology of the American Psychological Association, this series focuses on four major topics: counseling, career psychology, normal development/student development, and training and supervision. Each casebook includes four to six cases and delineates key topics. They also provide background and assessment information with actual dialogue from counseling sessions (all cases are edited and disguised with participants' consent). Authors also provide commentary alerting the reader to new concepts, where appropriate.

1. **Organizational Consultation**
   by **Robert K. Conyne & James M. O'Neil**

2. **Constructivist Assessment**
   by **Greg J. Neimeyer**

ORGANIZATIONAL CONSULTATION
A Casebook

edited by
ROBERT K. CONYNE
JAMES M. O'NEIL

THE COUNSELING PSYCHOLOGIST CASEBOOK SERIES

SAGE Publications
International Educational and Professional Publisher
Newbury Park   London   New Delhi

For information address:

SAGE Publications, Inc.
2455 Teller Road
Newbury Park, California 91320

SAGE Publications Ltd.
6 Bonhill Street
London EC2A 4PU
United Kingdom

SAGE Publications India Pvt. Ltd.
M-32 Market
Greater Kailash I
New Delhi 110 048 India

Printed in the United States of America

Library of Congress Cataloging-in-Publication Data

Main entry under title:
Organizational consultation: a casebook / edited by Robert K. Conyne,
    James M. O'Neil
            p.   cm.   —(The counseling psychologist casebook series; 1)
    Includes bibliographical references and index.
    ISBN 0-8039-4201-X (cl).   — ISBN 0-8039-4202-8 (pb)
    1. Psychological consultation—Case studies.   2. Organizational
behavior—Case studies.   I. Conyne, Robert K.   II. O'Neil, James M.
III. Series.
BF637.C56074   1992
158.7—dc20   92-20917

92   93   94   95   10   9   8   7   6   5   4   3   2   1

Sage Production Editor: Astrid Virding

We dedicate this book to all counseling psychologists who are or will become consultants, and to all other consultants who work to improve organizational effectiveness through the promotion of human development and healthy work enviroments for employees, colleagues, supervisors, and the people they serve.

Also, we dedicate this book to the ground-breaking, seminal work of Morrill, Oetting, and Hurst (1974), who developed the Counseling Cube Model. In the 1970's, these counseling psychologists and their colleagues from Colorado State University, along with those from a progressive number of institutions across the United States, created the conceptual foundation and applied application of consultation, mental health prevention, and training in Counseling Psychology that have continued to evolve over the last two decades.

Contents

Series Editor's Foreword

THE **Counseling Psychologist Casebook Series** is a response to the request of many readers of *The Counseling Psychologist* to provide more specific examples of the theories, concepts, and strategies described in that journal. It is the intent of this series that every year two or three casebooks will be published that will provide case examples of counseling approaches or problems that have previously been addressed as the major topic of an issue of *The Counseling Psychologist.* Casebooks will be most valuable, of course, when they address a topic for which it is most difficult to obtain extensive or closely supervised experience. As social learning theorists remind us, there is immense value in vicarious learning!

Given these considerations, it seems especially appropriate that the first casebook to be published is on the topic of organizational consultation. While the relationship of counseling psychology to consultation has been a topic of consideration in major articles and books in counseling psychology for nearly 30 years, both neophyte and experienced psychologists often find themselves relatively unprepared for the varied and distinctively different vicissitudes of consultation in organizations as compared with those encountered in most counseling relationships. Since organizational consultation cases often take months or years to complete, one accumulates experience very slowly; moreover, as is clearly apparent in this casebook, such experiences come in incredibly diverse forms. Despite the wide range of consultation projects described in this book, the authors have identified common principles and strategies, the foundation of which can typically be found as part of counseling psychology training. It is common experience to enter a consultation project and feel that one has not been prepared for what is needed, yet on the completion of the project, readily recognize that the most beneficial interventions were related to the basic principles and strategies of counseling psychology. This casebook was therefore designed to close the existing gap between consultation practice and training in counseling. *Organizational Consultation: A Casebook* provides a framework that will be valuable for both students and practitioners in understanding how to become more effective consultants. A unique and especially valuable feature of this casebook on consultation is the inclusion of the consultants' personal reactions to the cases they describe.

The editors, Robert K. Conyne and James M. O'Neil, have assembled a very highly experienced set of consultants to prepare the five cases in this book. The profession of counseling psychology owes them a debt of gratitude for their willingness to be the pioneers in this casebook series.

Finally, I wish to acknowledge, on behalf of the present and future readers of the casebook series, the contributions of C. Terry Hendrix, Vice President and Editorial Director of Sage Publications, who recognized readers' requests for casebooks and urged the editorial board of *The Counseling Psychologist* to undertake such an endeavor. The editorial board, now under the leadership of editor Gerald Stone, continues to be keenly interested in assisting all those who are interested in preparing proposals for future casebooks.

—BRUCE R. FRETZ
Series Editor, 1990-1992

Preface

ROBERT K. CONYNE

JAMES M. O'NEIL

Organization of the Casebook

THIS casebook consists of seven chapters, with its centerpiece being the five case studies. In addition to this introductory chapter, Chapters 2 through 6 contain the case studies. Chapter 7 contains an analysis and synthesis of the cases.

The authors of these case studies have been carefully selected. Each of them has produced a demonstrable track record of successful organizational consultation, including the cases recorded in this book. Their consultation experiences span a broad array of organizational settings, affording an impressive variety for examination and study. Each of them shares with the editors the human-development ideology of consultation, that it is a cyclical, collaborative, problem-solving process that seeks to assist a consultee or consultee system to improve role effectiveness. Their case studies illustrate the major elements of that perspective, while simultaneously capturing the uniqueness inherent in each situation. The fact that these authors include not only counseling psychologists but also professionals drawn from related disciplines, such as school psychology and health promotion, adds increased diversity and generalizability to the material.

We hope that this case study book will contribute to increasing the involvement of counseling psychologists and other helping professionals in the consultation enterprise.

To aid the reader in comparing and contrasting the five case studies, each of them has been written following the same organizational structure. The material in each case proceeds by first describing the consultation *background,* and then considering the consultation *issue(s), plan, implementation,* and *evaluation.* This organizational structure for the cases further reinforces the problem-solving steps that characterize consultation.

In addition, we have striven to make the case studies lively and real. Whenever possible, the cases contain examples of dialogue taken from the actual situation, or accurate reminiscences of it, so that the reader can get a very good sense of what actually transpired.

Moreover, the authors have reflected on the personal learnings they derived from their consultation experiences. We asked them to include not only success stories within their case studies, but also the difficulties with which they had to cope. As in any complex helping endeavor, and perhaps even more so with consultation, it almost rarely goes smoothly and predictably, despite the best efforts at planning. Consultation challenges can bring pleasant surprises and unwanted setbacks. We believe reading these cases will be useful and instructive to students in training, as well as to practicing consultants. Of course, the case materials are disguised appropriately and the permission of consultees has been obtained in every case study presented.

The Cases

Each of the case studies presents a retrospective analysis of what occurred. Although we selected the cases because they exemplified a collaborative problem-solving approach to long-term organizational consultation, the consultants may not have articulated their approach precisely in those terms while they actually were conducting their respective consultations. Therefore, explicit identification of the core concepts and premises used in this book came after the fact. We believe that interested readers can increase their consultation effectiveness substantially by conceptualizing their cases before the fact, during the evolution of their work. This entire book was developed to encourage consultants to conceptualize cases more actively during the early phases of contracting and entry into consultee systems.

In Chapter 1, we establish the conceptual framework and structure for the casebook by discussing the status of consultation, using counseling psychology as a model from which to generalize. We focus on the human-development consultation ideological system and develop a related set of consultation premises that are used to guide the five cases. These premises present an innovative approach to examining relationships existing between consultation ideological systems and roles. We indicate clearly the purpose for the casebook: To contribute to the advancement of consultation practice and training.

In Chapter 2, Lynn S. Rapin describes and analyzes a three-year organization consultation with an at-risk human service agency. She shows how the consultation progressed from a short-term, specific focus to a long-term, multifaceted organizational consultation.

In Chapter 3, Joseph E. Zins discusses a five-year school consultation and the difficulties he overcame in developing, expanding, institutionalizing, and evaluating the effort. This case will emphasize how a limited range of psychological services was broadened to include organizational consultation, as well as how consultation became an integral part of the educational delivery system of the school.

In Chapter 4, David A. Fravel and James M. O'Neil examine a two-year effort to produce and solidify change within a highly competitive and turbulent corporate environment. Human-development consultation approaches were used to address such issues as poor morale, insufficient training, confusion about performance standards, and the absence of a clear organizational vision.

In Chapter 5, Donald I. Wagner and Steven P. Krakoff probe a two-year consultation, of their own design, to assist an urban not-for-profit hospital system to develop and implement an overall strategic planning process for the creation of health promotion services. A Management Study Group for Health Promotion was formed, with which they worked collaboratively to design, implement, and evaluate this complex project.

In Chapter 6, James M. O'Neil and Robert K. Conyne describe and examine a three-year consultation conducted at a large, complex university that sought to reduce institutionalized racism and sexism. Their approach incorporated both advocacy and process consultation models and centered on the facilitation of system change amidst a host of challenging barriers.

In Chapter 7, the authors identify similarities and differences inherent across the five case studies. They give particular attention to recurring processes that would seem to hold special implications for research, training, and practice for counseling psychologists and other helping professionals who are involved with organizational consultation. The authors also highlight elements of the personal reflections they share and that would appear to provide special instructional benefit for readers.

1

Closing the Gap Between Consultation Training and Practice

ROBERT K. CONYNE

JAMES M. O'NEIL

A noticeable discrepancy exists in the helping professions between consultation practice and consultation training. On the one hand, professional helpers trained in a number of disciplines have become increasingly active as consultants (O'Neill & Trickett, 1982; Platt & Wicks, 1979). Psychology, counseling, social work, special education, and student personnel have endorsed the consultant role as central to their professional missions. However, professional preparation programs in these disciplines historically have devoted limited attention to consultation training (e.g., see Curtis & Meyers, 1988, Curtis & Zins, 1981b, and Gutkin & Curtis, 1990 in school psychology; Delworth, Hanson, & Associates, 1989 in student affairs; Idol-Maestas, 1983 and Idol, Paolucci-Whitcomb, & Nevin, 1986 in special education; and Kadushin, 1977 in social work). Within counseling psychology, the focal specialization of this book, the discrepancy between consultation practice and training is clearly evident (Bardon, 1985; Meade, Hamilton, & Yuen, 1982).

Many practitioners have approached consultation through the conceptual lenses of the dominant delivery systems of their profession, for example,

1

testing and assessment for school psychologists and counseling and psycho-therapy for counseling and clinical psychologists. As a result, much consultation is delivered by practitioners using models and skills adapted from related areas, but not drawn directly from concepts in the consultation literature.

Our purpose in organizing this casebook is to contribute to the advancement of training, practice, and research in consultation, with particular attention given to consultation in organizations. The casebook is directed to professional practitioners and students in the helping professions, broadly conceived: Counseling psychology, school psychology, counseling, social work, health promotion, clinical psychology, student personnel, special education, industrial organizational, and the like.

In this introductory chapter, we anchor our historical and contextual analysis of consultation to counseling psychology, due to space considerations and in recognition of the sponsorship of the casebook series by the Division of Counseling Psychology of the American Psychological Association (APA). It is important to realize, however, that the divergent consultation literature suggests that the place occupied by consultation in counseling psychology can be generalized to many other helping professions.

We are especially interested in fostering a closer linkage between the practice of consultation and the training appropriate to its proper execution. We draw from the important contributions to the consultation literature of Gallessich (1983, 1985) and others (e.g., Alpert, 1982; Alpert & Meyers, 1983; Blake & Mouton, 1986; Brown, Pryzwansky, & Schulte, 1987; Conoley & Conoley, 1982; Dustin & Blocher, 1984; Goodstein, 1978; Kurpius, 1985; Kurpius & Robinson, 1978; Lippitt & Lippitt, 1986; Mannino & Shore, 1985; Parsons & Meyers, 1984). We extend that literature by adding a framework for conceptualizing consultation that is based on the principles of human-development consultation (Gallessich, 1985) as applied to organizations, and by providing five comprehensive, detailed case studies supplemented by the identification of themes emerging across the cases.

The Gap Between Consultation Training and Practice

The Community Mental Health Act of 1963, and its call for consultation and education services in the community, illustrated one force that demanded a further response from counseling psychologists and other helping professionals. This legislation recommended interventions that expanded the traditional one-to-one "counseling services paradigm" (Conyne, 1987). Forces such as these had led Hurst (in Whiteley, 1980) to observe:

> "Counseling" is but one of many interventions we now have in our professional repertoire. We are now able to talk about training, *consultation* (italics ours), media . . . to mention just a few intervention strategies. It was never intended that "counseling," which is a process, should become an outcome to be perceived as an end in itself. (p. 198)

Yet, while counseling psychologists (and other helping professionals) did indeed *talk* about other interventions, such as consultation, professional roles and training remained unchanged. Counseling psychology found itself in a state of ambivalence, push-pulled between adhering closely to the "tried-and-true" formula of individual-remedial-direct service interventions (counseling and psychotherapy) or moving directly to add consultation and other interventions to its training, service, and research repertoire. As one result of this ambivalence, consultation in counseling psychology remains characterized by underdeveloped training, uneven practice, and a gap between practice and training.

In terms of consultation practice, one survey of American Psychological Association Division 17 members indicated that counseling psychologists spend about 15% of their time consulting (Nutt, 1976), while a more recent survey (Watkins, Lopez, Campbell, & Himmel, 1986) found that 61% of those counseling psychologists sampled spent an average 7.3% of their work week consulting. This latter percentage is an insubstantial fraction of the average 46 hours per week worked. Yet it is well beyond the percentage of time reported to be spent on such counseling psychology "staples" as vocational counseling (4.5%), vocational assessment (2.2%), and structured groups (2.4%). Of course, the 7.3% of time spent on consultation falls far short of the predominant intervention of contemporary counseling psychologists, individual psychotherapy (27.5%).

In terms of consultation training, surveys show consistent and disappointing results. A survey conducted by McNeill and Ingram (1983) of training directors of both APA- and non-APA-approved internship sites and programs, examined training practices in counseling psychology. Results of this survey showed that consultation techniques and consultation practicum are experienced by only a "few" students. These researchers conclude from their overall survey results that, "techniques of consultation appear to be given more precedence in internship settings than in graduate training programs" (p. 95).

Problems in consultation training are not new. Banikiotes (1977) found that most doctoral programs in counseling psychology weighted their curricula toward counseling theory, group process, assessment, and vocational development, with consultation and outreach ranking 20th in curricular offerings. Nearly a decade later, Birk and Brooks (1986) sampled 300 recent graduates in counseling psychology to determine which activities and competencies were important for effective job performance and to what extent doctoral training programs provided adequate training in those areas. Forty-nine percent of the respondents who rated consultation as important did not rate their training in it as adequate. In combination, survey results of consultation practice and training in counseling psychology indicate that a wide discrepancy exists between consultation practice, which appears to be relatively frequent, and consultation training, which seems to be both inadequate and infrequent.

Emerging signs exist, however, that the profession is beginning to face its ambivalence about consultation through its published standards, position papers, and more contemporary training practices. The "Specialty Guidelines for Delivery of Services by Counseling Psychologists" (American Psychological Association, 1981) include consultation as part of a counseling psychologist's services. Even more indicative of the emerging importance of consultation are current curricular advances in the intervention. Gallessich and Watterson (1984) found two thirds of the APA-accredited predoctoral training programs in counseling psychology offered an organized consultation course and 30% of these programs required this course. Over the last decade or so more published literature has appeared on consultation than ever before (e.g., Brown & Kurpius, 1985; Brown, Kurpius, & Morris, 1988; Dougherty, 1990; Dustin & Blocher, 1984; Gallessich, 1985; Hansen, Himes, & Meier, 1990; Kurpius, 1978; Kurpius & Brown, 1988; Kurpius, Dunn, & Brack, 1989; Hamilton & Meade, 1979; Leonard, 1977; Meade, Hamilton, & Yuen, 1982).

When many leaders in counseling psychology met for the Third National Conference for Counseling Psychology (Gazda, Rude, & Weissberg, 1988), consultation was included in several of the position papers. For example, Meara and associates (1988) listed consultation as one of eight content areas comprising the core of counseling psychology. Kagan and associates (1988) listed consultation as a major role and function of counseling psychologists working in a variety of settings including hospitals

(Altmaier, 1987), business and industry (Dowd, 1987), university counseling centers (Vasquez, 1987), and private practice (Tanney, 1987). Furthermore, it was recommended that counseling psychology training programs encourage diverse training opportunities through additional practica, placements, and specialized training in consultation (Kagan et al., 1988).

All of these developments suggest a growing commitment in counseling psychology to consultation, both in principle and practice. Simultaneously, a continuing and considerable need exists for advancing consultation training and practice in counseling psychology, because systematic and comprehensive preparation remains problematic. We believe this situation applies generally to most helping professions.

Toward Closing the Gap Between Training and Practice

The gap needs to be closed between the relatively large number of counseling psychologists and other professional helpers consulting and the relatively few who have received explicit training in consultation. At the very least, more graduate students need to receive formal training in consultation as an integral part of their graduate programs. While this is an obvious and straightforward statement, its accomplishment is fraught with entanglements. Graduate curricula are tightly regimented and usually little flexibility exists. Competing arguments for inclusion of courses addressing other undersubscribed but prescribed interventions, such as group counseling, can and should be made. Faculty who have themselves benefited from formal training in consultation may be limited in number. Resources available for program expansion are shrinking and, as mentioned already, what is included presently may be perceived as being absolutely necessary and largely immutable. Little or no room may exist for venturing into newer and underdeveloped areas. Therefore, for these and perhaps other reasons, tough professional and political decisions underlie the quest to increase the training in consultation in professional preparation programs.

An equally vexing question is what constitutes adequate consultation training? Very few validated training models have been described and disseminated, and these are restricted mostly to mental health consultation. However, we have found some existing sources to be particularly useful (see, e.g., Alpert & Meyers, 1983; Brown, 1985; Conoley, 1981;

Gallessich, 1983; Parsons & Meyers, 1984) as we have considered questions associated with consultation training. Converging conceptualizations drawn from these sources, combined with our thinking and experience, indicate that preservice consultation training must include a carefully sequenced series of didactic knowledge, experiential practice, field-based experiences with actual clients and client groups, and supervision. Once the helping professional is in the field consulting, peer-mediated learning approaches can become very helpful and sustaining. A professional peer support group, in which a small number of consultants meet together to learn from and support each other, illustrates one form of the peer-mediated learning approach.

Systematic and sequenced training in consultation is required, when the goal is to develop competencies for effective practice (Conoley, 1981; Curtis & Zins, 1981b; Parsons & Meyers, 1984). In one model (Curtis & Zins, 1981a), the process begins with didactic instruction in content areas and extends to include instructor demonstrations and role playing simulations in class. In the laboratory, videotape replay is used, practice in real situations is provided, and ongoing supervision occurs. Careful and consistent integration of consultation should occur throughout the entire professional training program.

Although no aspects of this linked series of training steps can be minimized, it is perhaps the creation of excellent field-based settings for consultation practice where the deficit is the most glaring. Quality supervised practice is a critical culminating experience for consultation, replacing the "on-the-job" and "life experience" formats that tend to occur frequently (Curtis & Zins, 1981b). Ideally, practica and internship experiences in consultation should be accorded the same status enjoyed by the "bread-and-butter" delivery systems of counseling and psychotherapy or of testing and assessment. Consultation competencies learned in training must be exercised in real settings with real cases, under watchful and qualified on-site and university supervision. In this way, the importance of embedding consultation appropriately within the ecology of a particular setting can be learned to counter any tendency toward viewing consultation as a preset package of technical skills to be routinely applied (O'Neill & Trickett, 1982). As well, trainees can learn how to apply self-managed behavioral change principles in order to monitor and manage their consultation practice directly (Wilson, Curtis, & Zins, 1987). We are nowhere near this level of training now, and moving in that direction presents many challenges.

However, the basic consultation training "road map" is available, as indicated through the material above. Competencies, such as in knowledge, behavior, and judgment, have been specified. Training modalities, such as through didactic presentations, experiential practice, self-managed behavior change, and field-based delivery, have been identified. The process of supervising consultation according to its evolving temporal sequence has been elucidated. The need for establishing credible field-based consultation sites has been emphasized. Two main challenges remain to be met: (a) expanding this generic training regimen beyond mental health consultation to other forms, such as organization consultation, work that Gallessich (1983) has begun and to which we contribute in this book; and (b) incorporating this training into existing graduate programs. The latter challenge appears to be the more formidable, for the reasons we have cited.

Relationship Between
Ideological Systems and Consultant Roles

The conceptual framework for consultation that we have developed governs each of the five case studies contained in the book. It originates with the three ideological systems of consultation presented by Gallessich (1985): (a) Human-development consultation, where human growth and development goals dominate; (b) Scientific-technological consultation, where the scientific method guides the intervention and information and principles are expertly provided; and (c) Social/political consultation, where political and social advocacy receive high priority.

The cases included in this book center on the application of the human-development ideological system to organizational consultation, with an emphasis on the collaborative approach. At the same time, we recognize that sometimes the most effective way to assist consultees is to provide expert advice, information, and direction (from the scientific-technological system), or to advocate a particular course of action reflecting the mutually espoused values of consultant and consultee (from the social/political system).

This blending of aspects from the three ideological systems within a single consultation reinforces the observation of Gallessich (1985), who indicated that the three systems she proposed may not be mutually exclusive. Although they represent unique ideological positions for conceptualizing

TABLE 1.1 Flexible Relationship Between Consultant Systems and Roles

Consultation System	Consultation Roles	
	Dominant	Secondary
Human-Development	Joint Problem Solver	Information Expert
		Advocate
Scientific-Technological	Information Expert	Joint Problem Solver
		Advocate
Social/Political	Advocate	Joint Problem Solver
		Information Expert

consultation, each system can accommodate consultation roles drawn judiciously from the other two systems. We propose that consultation can be understood more fully by recognizing that an interaction occurs between ideological systems and consultation roles.

Lippitt and Lippitt (1986) provided special assistance in considering consultation roles. They identified several roles as ranging along a continuum. We highlight three consultation roles on this continuum to illustrate the relationship between consultant roles and consultation systems:

- Joint Problem Solver role (Human-development system);
- Informational Expert role (Scientific-technological system);
- Advocate role (Social/political system).

We suggest that a dominant consultant role is associated with each system, such as joint problem solver with the human-development ideological system. However, we view the relationship existing between consultation systems and roles to be flexible and adaptive. Therefore, a human-development consultant can incorporate roles drawn from the two other systems, such as information expert or advocate, when it would serve to enhance overall consultation effectiveness.

This dynamic relationship between consultation systems and roles can be shown, and is described in Table 1.1.

As a reading of the cases in this book will demonstrate, roles drawn from the scientific-technological and social/political ideological systems may be involved in any one consultation. Let us refer briefly to just two cases, for illustration. In the case of O'Neil and Conyne on the change of racist and sexist institutional structures, the provision of expert information and the application of political processes were meshed within the human-development consultation to produce necessary system-wide changes. In her consultation with a social service organization, Rapin showed how providing expert assistance in strategic planning augmented her capacity to engage in joint collaborative problem solving with the consultee. Other human-development consultations included in this casebook uniquely weaved their own relationships among roles.

Conceptual Framework

Human-Development Consultation Ideology

Of the three ideological system we have discussed, *human-development consultation* is most consistent with what we perceive as a central value orientation of counseling psychology: to empower growth and development in human systems, whether the system be an individual, group, or organization. As Gallessich (1985) described human-development consultation:

> The highest priority of this system is human growth and development. Problems are conceptualized in terms of consultees' professional and personal developmental needs. Within this system are two different assumptions as to how to assist this development. These assumptions lead to different processes and roles. The therapeutic approach assumes that consultation will be most effective if the consultant takes responsibility for assessing and intervening in ways that will enhance the development of both the consultee and the organization. The *collaborative* (emphasis added) approach assumes that consultation will be more effective if consultant and consultee together assess the problem and evolve solutions to it. Underlying both approaches are assumptions that growth involves affective and cognitive processes and that the consultant's primary roles are educational and facilitative. (pp. 346-347)

We have adapted and extended this broad definition of the human-development consultation system, emphasizing the collaborative approach. We have identified four basic consultation premises to guide the cases reported in this book: (a) Consultation is a cyclical, collaborative problem-solving process; (b) Consultation is provided to a consultee or consultee system to advance role effectiveness, so that both the client is served more proficiently and consultee or consultee system functioning is enhanced;

(c) Organizational settings are a human system offering enormous consultative potential for empowering human development and prevention, and a systemic conception of organizations is especially well-suited for this work; and (d) Long-term consultations afford the maximal opportunity for providing enduring change. A discussion of each premise follows.

Adapted Premises
Underlying Human-Development Consultation

(a) *Cyclical, collaborative problem-solving processes are vital to human-development consultation.* Although the therapeutic approach to human-development consultation offers many benefits and needs to be included in the consultant's repertoire, the collaborative approach most fully exemplifies the ethos of empowerment, facilitation, and education that undergirds counseling psychology and many other helping professions. A cyclical, collaborative problem-solving approach explicitly demands that consultants and consultees develop a mutually satisfying procedure for working together (see Erchul, 1987; Witt, 1990) in order to: identify operating beliefs and vision that guide behavior (Kurpius, 1991), define the problem, generate potential solutions to it, design a problem solution plan for implementation, evaluate the effectiveness of that plan, and to recycle feedback along the way as appropriate. When used effectively, collaborative problem solving can involve consultees actively in a wide range of change processes and considerations. Although we believe this approach provides the best opportunity for counseling psychologists and other professional helpers to be effective as consultants in empowering human development and promoting prevention, we agree with Witt (1990) that any such claims about the collaborative method await substantiation through outcome studies.

(b) *Human-development consultation is delivered to a consultee or consultee system to advance role effectiveness, so that both the client is served more proficiently and consultee or consultee system functioning is enhanced.* One of the unique powers of consultation is its indirect service delivery, triadic structure, and its concomitant focus on effective performance of roles, work, and tasks. Clarity about these factors is necessary for practitioners to differentiate consultation from the array of direct services, such as counseling. In counseling, for instance, the counselor or therapist works directly with the client to help him or her resolve a personal concern. This process is a direct service, dyadic in structure and personally focused. In contrast, consultation is generally conceived of as an indirect service, triadic in structure, and work focused. The consultant assists a consultee (or consultee system, such as the management of an organization) to help resolve a role, work, or task issue the consultee is experiencing with a client. The consultant usually does not work directly with the client, but indirectly through the consultee, following a triadic structure: Consultant —Consultee—Client. Through such an approach, the consultant can aid the client or client system indirectly while also helping the consultee to apply learnings for enhanced role effectiveness in similar future situations.

(c) *Organizational settings are a human system offering enormous consultative potential for empowering human development and prevention, and a systemic conception of organizations is especially well-suited for this work.* Organizations are systems that strongly influence the behavior and attitudes of employers, employees, and consumers. For instance, the culture of an organization, represented by its shared values, beliefs, expectations, norms, and assumptions (Kilmann, 1989) has been shown to exert a pervasive and powerful continuing force on all phases of organizational life, including the processes of working and the outputs that result. Consultation to organizations that focuses on deep change, such as facilitating a positive cultural transformation (Porras & Silvers, 1991), can lead to extensive effects at multiple levels of the system.

Space fails to permit a complete definition of organization or of the organizational components amenable to human development consultation. However, in brief, it is useful to conceptualize an organization as an interrelated, interactive system of parts (Kuhn & Beam, 1982; Kurpius, 1989; Porras & Silvers, 1991; Weisbord, 1976). For instance (Porras & Silvers, 1991), the systemic components of an organization that are amenable to consultation include its arrangements (e.g., goals, strategies, structure), social factors (e.g., culture, interaction processes), technology (e.g., job design, technical system), and physical setting (e.g., space configuration, physical ambience). The cases described in this book show how counseling psychologists and other professional helpers can initiate, develop, and maintain long-term consultation projects in organizations by working with various subsystems and their interrelationships. Thereby, the cases practically illustrate the importance of locating organizational consultation within a general systemic conceptual model. As well, the cases illustrate some of the range of organizational types and settings where consultation can be occurring, such as health care, education, and corporate environments.

These organizational settings, with their largely untapped potential for fostering human development and prevention, may very well still constitute a "new frontier" for counseling psychology and other individually directed disciplines. However, organizational consultation has been discussed previously by counseling psychologists, recently in the Third National Conference for Counseling Psychology (Kagan et al., 1988) and before that, as well (e.g., Cochran, 1982, on organizational consultation on college campuses; Conyne et al., 1977, on consulting with organizational and environmental settings; Hamilton & Meade, 1979, and Kurpius, 1985, on adopting a systems view to consultation; Osipow & Toomer, 1982, on consulting in business and industry; and Rapin, 1985, and Thoresen & Eagleston, 1985, on consulting in health care settings). This "new frontier" is ripe for exploration by counseling psychologists and other helpers who are well trained in consultation.

(d) *Long-term human-development consultations afford the best opportunity for promoting enduring change in organizations.* We selected the five cases presented in this book carefully, in part because of their systematic attention to all phases of consultation: contact, contract, problem identification, goal setting, action and feedback, and termination (Lippitt & Lippitt, 1986). Accordingly, common terminology is used by the authors to explain the complex consultation processes in each case. Presentation of this information will provide readers with a recurring structure to understand how the cases were initiated, implemented, and evaluated over the lengthy duration of each consultation. Although short-term consultations are important, sometimes critically necessary, and can be very effective, our biases are that long-term consultation affords the greater possibility for attaining enduring change, especially in organizations.

Additionally, we think consultation occurring over a substantial period of time naturally provides a richness of data for exploration and in-depth analysis. We hope the cases described in detail in this casebook will contribute to improved practice, training, and research in consultation.

References

Alpert, J. (Ed.). (1982). *Psychological consultation in educational settings.* San Francisco: Jossey-Bass.

Alpert, J., & Meyers, J. (Eds.). (1983). *Training in consultation: Perspectives from mental health, behavioral and organizational consultation.* Springfield, IL: Charles C Thomas.

Altmaier, E. (April, 1977). *Practice role in hospital medical settings.* Paper presented at the National Conference for Counseling Psychology, Atlanta, GA.

American Psychological Association. (1981). Specialty guidelines for the delivery of services by counseling psychologists. *American Psychologist, 36,* 652-663.

Banikiotes, P. (1977). The training of counseling psychologists. *The Counseling Psychologist, 7,* 79-81.

Bardon, J. (1985). On the verge of a breakthrough. In D. Brown & D. Kurpius (Eds.), Consultation [Special issue], *The Counseling Psychologist, 13,* 355-362.

Birk, J., & Brooks, L. (1986). Required skills and training needs of recent counseling psychology graduates. *Journal of Counseling Psychology, 33,* 320-325.

Blake, R., & Mouton, J. (1986). *Consultation.* Reading, MA: Addison/Wesley.

Brown, D. (1985). The preservice training and supervision of consultants. In D. Brown & D. Kurpius (Eds.), Consultation [Special issue], *The Counseling Psychologist, 13,* 410-425.

Brown, D., & Kurpius, D. (Eds). (1985). Consultation [Special issue]. *The Counseling Psychologist, 13*(3).

Brown, D., Kurpius, D., & Morris, J. (Eds.). (1988). *Handbook of consultation with individuals and small groups* (Order No. 72295). Washington, DC: Association for Counselor Education and Supervision.

Brown, D., Pryzwansky, W., & Schulte, A. (1987). *Psychological consultation.* Boston: Allyn & Bacon.

Cochran, D. (1982). Organizational consultation: A planning group approach. *Personnel and Guidance Journal, 60,* 314-317.

Conoley, J. (1981). *Consultation in schools.* New York: Academic Press.

Conoley, J., & Conoley, C. (1982). *School consultation.* Elmsford, NY: Pergamon.

Conyne, R. (1987). *Primary preventive counseling: Empowering people and systems.* Muncie, IN: Accelerated Development.

Conyne, R., Banning, J., Clack, R., Corazzini, J., Huebner, L., & Wrenn, R. (August, 1977). *The environment as client: Considerations and implications for counseling psychology.* Paper presented at the annual meeting of the American Psychological Association, San Francisco.

Curtis, M., & Meyers, J. (1988). Consultation: A foundation for alternative services in the schools. In J. Zins & M. Curtis (Eds.), *Alternative educational delivery systems: Enhancing instructional options for all students* (pp. 35-48). Washington, DC: National Association of School Psychologists.

Curtis, M., & Zins, J. (March, 1981a). *The experiential component in training for consultation.* Paper presented at the annual meeting of the National Association for School Psychologists, Houston, TX.

Curtis, M., & Zins, J. (1981b). *The theory and practice of school consultation*. Springfield, IL: Charles C Thomas.

Delworth, U., Hanson, G., & Associates. (Eds.). (1989). *Student services: A handbook for the profession* (2nd ed.). San Francisco: Jossey-Bass.

Dougherty, A. (1990). *Consultation: Practice and perspectives*. Pacific Grove, CA: Brooks/Cole.

Dowd, E. (April, 1987). *Counseling psychology in business and industry*. Paper presented at the National Conference for Counseling Psychology, Atlanta, GA.

Dustin, D., & Blocher, D. (1984). Consultation. In S. Brown & R. Lent (Eds.), *Handbook of counseling psychology*. New York: John Wiley.

Erchul, W. (1987). A relational communication analysis of control in school consultation. *Professional School Psychology, 2,* 113-124.

Gallessich, J. (1983). Training psychologists for consultation with organizations. In J. Alpert & J. Meyers (Eds.), *Training in consultation* (pp. 142-163). Springfield, IL: Charles C Thomas.

Gallessich, J. (1985). Toward a meta-theory of consultation. In D. Brown & D. Kurpius (Eds.), Consultation [Special issue], *The Counseling Psychologist, 13,* 336-354.

Gallessich, J., & Watterson, J. (1984). *Consultation education and training in APA-accredited settings: An overview*. Paper presented at the 92nd annual meeting of the American Psychological Association, Toronto, Canada.

Gazda, G., Rude, S., & Weissberg, M. (Ed.). (1988). Third National Conference for Counseling Psychology: Planning the future [Special issue]. *The Counseling Psychologist, 16.*

Goodstein, L. (1978). *Consulting with human services systems*. Reading, MA: Addison-Wesley.

Gutkin, T., & Curtis, M. (1990). School-based consultation: Techniques and research. In T. Gutkin & C. Reynolds (Eds.), *The handbook of school psychology* (2nd. ed., pp. 577-611). New York: John Wiley.

Hamilton, M., & Meade, C. (Eds.). (1979). *Consulting on campus*. San Francisco: Jossey-Bass.

Hansen, J., Himes, B., & Meier, S. (1990). *Consultation: Concepts and practices*. Englewood Cliffs, NJ: Prentice-Hall.

Idol, L., Paolucci-Whitcomb, P., & Nevin, A. (1986). *Collaborative consultation*. Rockville, MD: Aspen.

Idol-Maestas, L. (1983). *Special educators: Consultation handbook*. Rockville, MD: Aspen.

Kadushin, A. (1977). *Consultation in social work*. New York: Columbia University Press.

Kagan, N., & Associates. (1988). Professional practice of counseling psychology in various settings. *The Counseling Psychologist, 16,* 347-365.

Kilmann, R. (1989). *Managing beyond the quick fix*. San Francisco: Jossey-Bass.

Kuhn, A., & Beam, R. (1982). *The logic of organization: A system-based social science framework for organization*. San Francisco: Jossey-Bass.

Kurpius, D. (1978). Consultation theory and practice: An integrated model. *Personnel and Guidance Journal, 56,* 335-338.

Kurpius, D. (1985). Consultation interventions: Successes, failures, and proposals. In D. Brown & D. Kurpius (Eds.), Consultation [Special issue], *The Counseling Psychologist, 13, 368-389.*

Kurpius, D. (1989). *A systems perspective for determining consultation interventions.* New York: National Education Association Publications.

Kurpius, D. (1991, May). *Three paradigms for helping: Cognitive mediation, consultation, and strategic planning.* Presentation at the University of Cincinnati, Cincinnati, OH.

Kurpius, D., & Brown, D. (Eds.). (1988). *Handbook of consultation: An intervention for advocacy and outreach* [Special issue]. Washington, DC: Association for Counselor Education and Supervision.

Kurpius, D., Dunn, L., & Brack, G. (1989). Alternative approaches to consultation practice. *Counseling and Human Development, 21,* 1-9.

Kurpius, D., & Robinson, S. (1978). An overview of consultation. *Personnel and Guidance Journal, 56,* 321-323.

Leonard, M. (1977). The counseling psychologist as an organizational consultant. *The Counseling Psychologist, 7,* 73-77.

Lippitt, G., & Lippitt, R. (1986). *The consulting process in action* (2nd ed.). La Jolla, CA: University Associates.

Mannino, F., & Shore, M. (1985). Understanding consultation: Some orienting dimensions. In D. Brown & D. Kurpius (Eds.), Consultation [Special issue], *The Counseling Psychologist, 13, 363-367.*

McNeill, B., & Ingram, J. (1983). Prevention and counseling psychology: A survey of training practices. *The Counseling Psychologist, 11,* 95-96.

Meade, C., Hamilton, K., & Yuen, R. (1982). Consultation research: The time has come, the walrus said. *The Counseling Psychologist, 10,* 39-51.

Meara, N., & Associates. (1988). Training and accreditation in counseling psychology. *The Counseling Psychologist, 16,* 366-384.

Nutt, R. (1976). A study of consultation services provided by counseling psychologists. *Dissertation Abstracts International, 37,* 5816B. (University Microfilms No. 77-9516,157)

O'Neill, P., & Trickett, E. (1982). *Community consultation.* San Francisco: Jossey-Bass.

Osipow, S., & Toomer, J. (Eds.). (1982). Counseling psychology in business and industry. *The Counseling Psychologist, 10.*

Parsons, R., & Meyers, J. (1984). *Developing consulting skills.* San Francisco: Jossey-Bass.

Platt, J., & Wicks, R. (1979). *The psychological consultant.* New York: Grune & Stratton.

Porras, J., & Silvers, R. (1991). Organizational development and transformation. *Annual Review of Psychology, 42,* 51-78.

Rapin, L. (1985). Organization development: Quality circle groups. In R. Conyne (Ed.), *The group workers' handbook: Varieties of group experience* (pp. 214-232). Springfield, IL: Charles C Thomas.

Tanney, M. (April, 1987). *Empowering counseling psychologists in private practice.* Paper presented at the National Conference for Counseling Psychology, Atlanta, GA.

Thoresen, C., & Eagleston, J. (Eds.). (1985). Counseling for health. *The Counseling Psychologist, 13.*

Vasquez, M. (April, 1987). *Diversity and multicultural counseling from a counseling psychologist's perspective: A reaffirmation.* Paper presented at the National Conference for Counseling Psychology, Atlanta, GA.

Watkins, C., Lopez, F., Campbell, V., & Himmel, C. (1986). Contemporary counseling psychology: Results of a national study. *Journal of Counseling Psychology, 33,* 301-309.

Weisbord, M. (1976). Organizational diagnosis: Six places to look for trouble with or without a theory. *Group and Organizational Studies, 1,* 430-447.

Whiteley, J. (1980). *The history of counseling psychology.* Monterey, CA: Brooks/Cole.

Wilson, F. R., Curtis, M., & Zins, J. (1987, August). *Consultant self-managed behavior change during consultation training.* Paper presented at the annual meeting of the American Psychological Association, New York.

Witt, J. (1990). Collaboration in school-based consultation: Myth in need of data. *Journal of Educational and Psychological Consultation, 1,* 367-370.

2

Consultation With a Human Service Agency: Improving Management Practices

LYNN S. RAPIN

THIS case study involves an at-risk human service agency. My work began with a specific, time-limited agency assessment and developed into a long-term, multifaceted organization development consultation. These consultations were delivered through two separately negotiated contracts, the first of these dealing with an organization assessment and the second dealing with implementation of the assessment recommendations. I did not anticipate at its onset that the consultation would become a four-year project. My retrospective account of the case follows the Conyne and O'Neil framework presented in Chapter 1 with its human-development, collaborative, and process emphases (Gallessich, 1985; Schein, 1969, 1987). While the consultation goals changed during the four-year process, the organizing principles remained constant with those I had been using during approximately 10 years of consultation practice.

Background and Consultation Issues

I was referred to a public funding board that was soliciting consultation for one of its many human service contract agencies. The potential consultee agency was not meeting compliance specifications and was in jeopardy of compromising or losing its major funding. After providing my credentials for review I was invited to submit a proposal for an agency assessment.

The funding board was assuming the cost of the assessment while jointly sponsoring it with the consultee agency and agency governing board. Proposals would be reviewed and approved by the agency, its board, and the funding board.

Potential consultants were provided a two-page document outlining assessment areas that had been identified in discussions among the agency director, the agency board chair, and senior staff of the funding board. Areas for exploration included the agency's basic mission, related goals, and organizational dynamics. Some specific concerns included large cost overruns requiring pay backs by both the funder and the agency, management's lack of awareness of reductions in intakes and clients served, numerous contract compliance problems, and strained relationships with other community care givers.

While all of the proposal development activities were undertaken on my own unreimbursed time, I felt that I needed to understand the perspectives of each participant group (the agency, its governing board, and the funder) to design a reasonable and competitive proposal. Therefore, I scheduled an informational meeting with the two key administrators of the funding board and requested any written materials that could assist me in understanding the agency's assessment needs prior to our meeting. I received copies of funding audits and minutes from agency and governing board meetings. In reviewing these documents I learned that a search for a consultant had been going on for eight months. I assumed that there might be agency resistance to consultation or confusion about potential consultation goals. I considered my initial meeting a critical entry activity that would influence any future consultation potential.

Through the exploratory interview and in reviewing the printed materials, I learned that the agency was experiencing acute cash flow and resource utilization problems. As well, many of the agency's problems were perceived by the funding board as chronic, only masked by a constant availability of emergency situations. The agency in question did not seem to be able to respond proactively to issues faced broadly in the large human service system.

After meeting with the funding board executives and reviewing materials that they had provided to me, I submitted a proposed plan for the consultation. I was one of three "finalist" consultants being considered for the contract.

Assessment Plan

The agency director and the funding board were concerned about the health of the agency, but they were not sure which factors were most problematic. One major goal of the assessment was to better understand what was really going on in the agency. My design was intended to clarify existing problems and strengths within the agency and to serve as a positive foundation for implementing constructive action.

My assessment design relied on the perceptions of the agency held by agency staff, governing board members, funding board members, and referral sources. I felt that the assessment results would be most valid if all participants had the opportunity to contribute to the generation of the information and to receive the results of the assessment. I wanted to propose an assessment design that would promote confidence in and commitment to the assessment process. Further, it was important that I define my role as consultant in a way that would keep me in a neutral position as I gathered information about the agency.

As I considered potential assessment components, I kept in mind the likelihood that financial resources would be somewhat limited. I recommended four data collection methods that would provide a comprehensive picture of the agency within a total budget of approximately 120 hours.

Interviews

Interviews were to be conducted with (a) agency administrators and staff, (b) agency governing board, (c) funding board administrators and key liaison staff to the agency, and (d) key referral sources. Program directors, central administrators, and funding board representatives were identified as key interviewees in my proposal. The plan stipulated that I would negotiate with the agency director and funding board executives the specific line staff, current and past governing board members, and appropriate referral sources to be interviewed.

Questionnaires

Based on interview data, a tailored questionnaire would be distributed to all governing board members. Because all delivery staff were individually interviewed and offered personal follow-up time, no further written input was deemed necessary from them.

Work Environment Scale

A standardized work climate questionnaire, the *Work Environment Scale* (Insel & Moos, 1974), would be administered to all agency staff in two forms, to identify both current perceptions and ideal/desired perceptions.

Support Documents

Relevant agency documents would be reviewed. These documents included staff meeting and governing board minutes, compliance audit reports, and funder-generated utilization studies.

Data Ownership and Reporting

My written proposal included the stipulation that all raw data would remain my property and that only group data would be shared with consultees. Written and oral assessment reports were to be provided jointly to the full funding board and its officers, to the agency governing board officers, and to appropriate agency administrators and staff. I recommended that staff members be provided assessment results because they were to be included in the information gathering process. Group themes, problem perceptions, and recommendations were to be presented in summary form. All assessment components and written and verbal reports were to be completed within three months of proposal acceptance.

One personal scheduling issue would affect the timing of the assessment and results presentation. I was expecting a baby in four months and wanted all of the data gathering and compilation of results to be completed by that time. I did not want to interrupt the assessment process. I concentrated my efforts, therefore, to guarantee that all components could be completed prior to my due date.

My proposal for the assessment of the agency was accepted in full by all parties including staff and administration of the agency, its governing board, and the funding board. A meeting was scheduled between the funding administrators, the agency director, governing board officer, and myself to initiate the consultation.

Contract One: Organization Assessment

Forming a Contract and Working Relationship

Six weeks elapsed between the submission of my proposal and the start of the consultation. At the initial meeting representing all parties, I met the agency director and the governing board vice-chair for the first time. Even though my proposal and credentials had been reviewed by each party during the selection process, I had the opportunity to meet personally only with funding board administrators prior to contract approval. I did not want this early contact to be interpreted as alignment with the funders and their perceptions of the problem.

The question of who initiated the consultation was to be a point of ownership and disagreement between the funding board and the agency that never really got resolved. Both the agency director and the funding board administrators perceived that they originated the consultation request. The funders perceived that it was their impetus that was driving the agency to seek consultation. In contrast, the agency director and governing board felt they had sought help on their own but had not found a suitable provider. I reinforced the positive initiative that both parties expressed, minimizing the conflict over who had the idea first.

I felt that collaboratively negotiating basic ground rules for the consultation with representatives of the key consultee groups would be essential to establishing trust at the critical entry stage of the consultation. It was imperative, therefore, for me to present and resolve potential political and ethical issues (Robinson & Gross, 1985) before any data were generated. Ground-rule subjects included definition of the consultee, consultant orientation, ownership of assessment data, use of data, and scheduling details.

It was important for me to understand and communicate consistently how we would define the consultee. It was agreed that the agency management was the consultee and that contacts with the funding board, agency governing board, agency staff, and other community agencies would be made to assist the managers of the agency in carrying out their responsibilities. This focus on management effectiveness remained constant during the four-year consultation as I worked with several levels of management (see Figure 2.1). Because the organization's structure changed during the consultation, both original and subsequent titles are provided in a final/original title format.

Additionally, I was concerned that I might become the messenger with very bad news. I wanted to provide accurate information about the organization and reduce any real or perceived job threat to the agency director or other personnel. I discussed with the group that the agency director would likely be identified as a major target, and that material generated about him might be very loaded and negative. In my past organization consultations and in other consultants' experiences (Walton & Warwick,

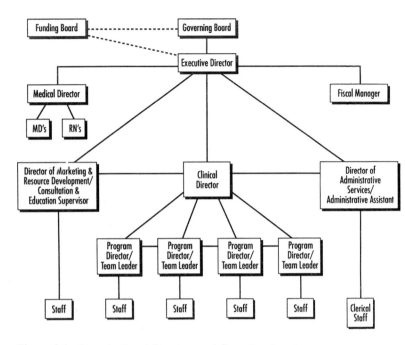

Figure 2.1. Organizational Structure and Consultee Levels

1973), merely looking at perceptions of problems could generate a good deal of criticism about the leadership of the organization. I wanted the director to feel safe during the exploration process. After discussion, all administrators agreed that the assessment results would not be used as a strategy to remove the agency leaders. This agreement was critical in that it reinforced the human-development opportunities of the assessment and ensured that my efforts would not be used to disguise administrative restructuring of the agency.

Collecting Assessment Data

While general categories of interviewees were identified in my proposal, final interviewees had to be selected. I wanted all of the administrators to trust in the data sources prior to the assessment. The funding board administrators, the agency management team, and I jointly determined that all service delivery staff, all full-time clerical staff, program managers, administrators, and former and current governing board chairs would be individually interviewed. Line staff were allocated one initial hour each, program leaders and management team members were allocated two initial hours, and the agency director four initial hours. All interviewees were given the opportunity for follow-up time. Lengthy follow-up was required with the director and clinical director.

I negotiated an interview sequence that allowed the agency director and management team members to share their perceptions first, followed by closely scheduled staff, board, and referral source interviews. All interviews were conducted on-site to limit intrusion in work calendars, minimize discussion of the assessment process among staff yet to be interviewed, and maximize the likelihood that interview data would reflect the agency at the same period in time.

Two *Work Environment Scale* (Insel & Moos, 1974) group administrations were scheduled to minimize discussion of the items and to capture perceptions at the same point in the assessment process.

Current agency governing board officers and one at-large member were interviewed as a group. Key referral sources, regardless of the positive or negative nature of their relationship with the agency, were jointly identified by funding executives and agency director for individual interviews. A total of 45 initial and follow-up interviews were conducted within seven weeks.

Tabulating and Disseminating Assessment Data

Each interview record and questionnaire was separately coded for content and process issues. Coded information was then integrated across all interviewees and organized around themes that consistently emerged from the data. No predetermined categories were employed.

Work Environment Scale results were scored and tabulated for each person, program, staff level, and whole agency. Individual results were prepared for each staff member for their private comparisons with group perceptions. Only group results were made available to funding board, agency administrators, governing board, and staff.

The themes I presented in the assessment report were the concerns that funding board and governing board members, agency administrators, staff, and referral sources consistently identified as critical to the effective functioning of the agency. Issues unique to one interviewee or to one administrative area were not presented.

The feedback schedule was designed to provide consistent and timely information to all levels of the agency and the two boards, and to minimize any discussion of the material prior to formal receipt of the results. The feedback schedule was set to begin after a 2 ½ week maternity break, so that there would be minimal lag between the data gathering and dissemination phases. While this proved to be a rigorous schedule for me, I felt that it was necessary to provide prompt feedback to all consultation participants. My schedule required that I plan my energy resources carefully, so that I would not be exhausted by the combination of work intensity and the demands and excitement of a new family member.

Individual feedback sessions were scheduled with the agency director and clinical program director because much of the content was directed at issues of their leadership and roles. While it was important to present the material about these two management positions in a straightforward manner in my formal reports, I felt it was imperative that they hear the material before public presentation.

Eight feedback presentations were made in the following sequence: (a) agency director, (b) funding board administrator, (c) full funding board and governing board officers, (d) agency clinical program director, (e) full management team, and (f) full agency staff, (g) full agency governing board, and (h) social climate results to full agency staff. Multiple presentations were scheduled on the same day (a through c; e and f) as schedules could accommodate.

The agency director was present at all sessions except during the individual feedback meeting with the funding board administrator. While I made essentially the same presentation of results each time, I thought that the director's presence would aid his absorption of the assessment information and communicate to all levels of staff and boards the director's willingness to work with the data.

Six major themes emerged from the assessment, each with content and process components: (a) communication, (b) planning and decision making, (c) trust, (d) role confusion, (e) resource allocation, and (f) staff burnout. Each theme area was described in summary detail in writing and presented in person to all major parties. Although labor intensive, formal verbal presentations allowed me to set the tone and context for the results and recommendations, and to enhance my already-established working relationships with the agency and boards.

Recommendations

I provided four specific written recommendations that the agency and the relevant boards could pursue in response to the assessment findings. In this consultant activity I used my familiarity with the assessment data to develop some potential next steps. While still operating in the human-development system, I was taking a more therapeutic approach in recommending specific foci for further consultation or intervention.

The recommendations were as follows.

1. Define specific agency goals and develop a set of implementation plans to carry out these goals. Concentrate on important, select areas for goal development.

2. Clarify or redefine major areas of responsibility within management and team leader ranks to better distribute resources and foster reestablishment of trust. Assess the fit between job descriptions, responsibilities, and adequate time required to accomplish job tasks successfully. Redistribute responsibilities accordingly. Focus on how structure can support rather than constrain the talents within the management and team leader groups.

3. Increase verbal and written information flow among agency administration and both boards to keep the data base current and information accurate. Have the funding board staff define what specific performance improvements must be made to enable the future survival of the agency and appropriate expansion of its programs.

4. Have the agency governing board become more involved with the agency. Start the involvement process with clearly defined goals (one- to five-year plans), support and direction for the agency director, and active dialog with the funding board. Take stronger positions and make planning decisions that move the agency from crisis intervention to long-range planning. Assume the role that had been informally taken by the funding board.

As part of the feedback process, I recommended that the agency use additional consultation to address the issues identified at assessment. It became clear in the initial consultation that correction of long-standing and potentially overwhelming problems was unlikely without additional help. Further, organization development through a longer term, collaborative, human-development effort (Conyne & O'Neil, 1990; Gallessich, 1985) seemed far more appropriate than a prescriptive, short-term intervention initially suggested by the funding administrator. When presented with this recommendation, the full funding board responded favorably.

They stated that they were impressed with the scope of the assessment and that further assistance seemed appropriate.

Bridging Contract

The funding board allocated approximately 65 hours of time during the next eight weeks for me to begin consulting with the agency while designing an implementation plan. In spite of its financial problems, the agency was willing to participate in funding continued consultation. The funding board was encouraged by this agency commitment, and requested a consultation proposal and time line for implementation of the assessment recommendations.

The funder requested that I not proceed too far with the process until a specific plan could be approved by the full funding board at a monthly meeting. At this point, the funding administrator had not yet decided whether to authorize a short-term or long-term consultation. Funding was to be determined on the strength of the plan submitted. This stipulation both provided me with the opportunity, and imposed some pressure on me, to secure the collaboration of the major consultees in the planning process.

I used my assessment recommendation that the agency define specific agency-level goals and strategies as the basis for the implementation plan. I was concerned that agency management could be overwhelmed by the scope and intensity of the assessment results. I wanted a plan that would help provide structure and support for the work that would follow. As well, a detailed plan would allow me to measure my own progress in the consultation process. I felt that an implementation plan collaboratively designed by the agency director, the governing board, and myself would be far more appropriate than any prescriptive plan that I might design. Further, this process would foster positive communication among the agency management, board, and funding administrators.

The agency director, governing board chair, and I formed a planning group (Moore & Delworth, 1976) to convert the assessment results into a formal planning document. Our proposal was then submitted to the funding board for formal approval.

As in the initial assessment contract, the funding board served as the fiscal executive and final decision maker for my consultation services to be delivered to the contract agency. I concluded that the funding board had to be involved in the receipt of future consultation in order to improve information flow and clarity of expectations with the agency. There were some loaded political issues in the fiscal relationship between the agency and the funder that had contributed to the agency's perceived problems. As with the assessment contract negotiation, I determined that it was essential for me to communicate my neutrality in regard to allegiance to either the funding board or the agency.

The implementation proposal, budgeting 320 hours of consultation for the next year, was reviewed by the funding board, revised, and submitted for final approval within six weeks. The plan included three agency goal areas related directly to the assessment results and recommendations.

The implementation plan was fully approved and financially supported by the funding board and the agency in a 90/10 proportion. The agency director and governing board determined with the funder what dollar figure would communicate the agency's investment in the improvement of the agency's management without unduly stressing their already bad financial situation. The agency director identified some internal funds that could be reallocated to the consultation effort. We disbanded the planning group upon approval of the implementation contract because both the agency director and governing board chair were to be recipients of further consultation.

As in the original assessment consultation contract, interview data were to remain my property so that I would have the freedom to use the material throughout the consultation. I did not want to get into a situation in which I could not appropriately use the information that was likely to be shared with me. To foster commitment to the change process and to reinforce the collaborative nature of the working relationship with me, I specified in the written implementation plan that participants would be strongly encouraged to share their perceptions and information directly with appropriate agency personnel, governing and funding boards, and referral sources and not depend upon me, the consultant, as their major information conduit.

Three specific agency goals were identified for implementing the assessment results. Each goal had specific objectives, strategies, target dates, and budgeted consultation time. Additionally, my role as consultant was described in each level of the plan. The goals were:

Goal I: To review, evaluate and modify the organizational and management structures of the agency.

Goal II: To define the ongoing functions and responsibilities of the agency board.

Goal III: To improve communication within the agency and in external relationships with the county board and referral sources.

Contract Two: Implementing Assessment Results

Contract two was constructed to follow-up on the assessment results.
The purpose of the continued consultation was to assist the agency in maintaining compliance with all regulatory policies and procedures through
consistent performance, based upon (a) sound planning, (b) accurate and
up-to-date communication and information flow, and (c) a more appropriately assertive management style. One concern of the funding board
was that the agency management might want me to do their work for them.
In their own experience with the agency, the funding board had found
itself rescuing the agency on many occasions. The funding board administrators felt that this was an inappropriate strategy on their part and did
not want me to enter into a similar relationship with the agency. I emphasized that the process of consultation would assist the agency in identifying and developing their own responses to problems so that the agency
would be less dependent upon emergency help in the future. I also told the
consultees that the process would move slowly, because long-established
patterns are not modified without careful analysis and practice. In essence, the consultation required changes in both attitude and behavior,
not only for the agency, but also for the governing and funding boards.

Year One Implementation

While I was working with the agency director and governing board
chair on the elements of the implementation proposal, I began the first
steps of the consultation with the agency's management. During the time
that the proposal was in preparation and review I had to be very careful
in the scope of my work with the management team. I selected with the
director one area to pursue prior to final proposal approval. This area of
exploration included the review and evaluation of management roles and
responsibilities. Clarification of these roles would assist the agency in either
a short-term consultation or in a longer organization development effort.

When the implementation plan for the management consultation was
formally approved, I was able to continue the work that I had begun with

the management team and begin working with the agency board. In funding 320 hours of consultation time over the next 12-month period, the funding board and agency committed to a developmental process to improve the agency's management practices. The funder's approval signaled an encouraging change in expectation for the agency's management.

Goal I focused on the agency structures. Much of my consultation time during the next six months was devoted to addressing this goal. Team-building activities were introduced to foster open communication among the four members of the administrative group, and to establish a level of trust required to address major problems. These team-building activities included defining conflicts, establishing cooperative work goals and ground rules, negotiating areas of responsibility, generating more appropriate personal responses to each other, and designing group responses to problems, as examples. The management team and I began to examine the agency's structure in light of the problems related to lack of clarity of leadership, inconsistency in follow-through, and poorly defined management team responsibilities.

The formal management team was perceived as dysfunctional, and two of its four members were not widely viewed as management staff. The roles of agency executive director and clinical program director were viewed as so confusing that many staff were unsure of who was truly running the agency. Further, the clinical director was seen as having a larger than desired span of control. Management team members were perceived as competing for control and position. The need for firmer and more consistent leadership, particularly at the executive level, was clear. These problems suggested that both structural and political aspects of the agency's management would have to be explored. Issues of power and influence were central to the concerns identified at the assessment.

I began meeting with the four-member management team to assist them in defining how they might work as a more functional administrative group and what each member might do to foster that end. The agency director, board chair, and I had determined, and the management team concurred, that it was essential to demonstrate progress in this problem area. The management group established a ground rule that they would not discuss the details of any potential redistributed job responsibilities until the appraisal and redesign process was complete. In this way, inappropriate information channels and miscommunications would be minimized.

In a series of intense meetings over a three-month period, the management team spent time describing their current functions as they were actually executed. Each member also described potential or desired responsibilities that they could assume in a more constructive management team. These were very painful meetings in which the failings and aspirations of each member of the management team were revealed to the group.

It was important from my perspective to encourage the group to visualize themselves in more productive roles so that they could move from the emergency response orientation they were experiencing at assessment. I facilitated the brainstorming exercises, guided force-field analyses, and kept written records of current and potential functions for each management position. The group then used the present/future comparisons in an integrated fashion to evaluate and redistribute job responsibilities. My role was to facilitate the group's exploration and encourage positive movement in the group. I concluded from the group's progress that they would be able to formulate a more effective management structure.

While I was working with the management group, I also began meeting independently with the agency director to assist with the issue of leadership style. In our early meetings, the director and I sorted through and synthesized the assessment results that related to whole-agency strengths and weaknesses. We then began to focus on those results that pertained to the director. As is often the case, the data regarding the director were very negative. I concentrated on assisting the director in moving from taking sweeping personal responsibility for all problems to identifying specific aspects of leadership style that could be modified. It was painful for the director to confront personal style issues that were perceived as hindering the agency.

In retrospect, some of my most critical consultation activities during the first six months of implementation seem very simple to me. These included gathering the members of the management team together for long enough time periods (generally two hours) so that they could talk together about the problems facing the agency. The program areas providing direct services were small and had been managed with little coordination. The group had not really looked at the organization as a system in a comprehensive, developmental way. The management team and staff had focused on delivering quality human services to a growing population but had few measures of program effectiveness or efficiency.

Past practice had involved angry, solitary responses from members of the management team as well as protective responses for themselves and the director. I worked with the group to consider the forces that were hindering their effectiveness. The management team was able to identify issues of competition and specific interpersonal conflicts within the group and to negotiate with me a plan for addressing long-standing hostilities. I worked independently with specific members of the management team and collaboratively planned with them steps for improved communication and trust building. Members were able to negotiate specific changes in behavior toward each other that they felt would enhance their effectiveness. Rather than identifying these concerns to the group, I focused my attention on building a climate in which they could discuss the issues themselves. One of the values of the human-development orientation that I held was that the management group had the potential of identifying barriers to effectiveness and that, with consultation, the group could design appropriate and effective responses.

This series of meetings fostered trust in me and greatly added to the working ability of the management group. Members of management were concerned that they might be sacrificial lambs in the change process and were relieved when they were able to move beyond old barriers to cooperation. The facilitated management discussions both encouraged the group as they redefined responsibilities and priorities and served as a model for their interactions with other staff. My own training and experience in group facilitation was essential to any success I had with the group.

Once the management team explored various aspects of its current and future roles and responsibilities, I conducted a series of exercises to assist them in considering potential modifications to the structure of the agency. For example, I had the group imagine different configurations for the agency and use the strengths of each idea to generate a more realistic organization structure. The organization was redesigned to streamline information flow, to group cognitively similar programs together under one mid-management team leader, to reduce the number of programs reporting to the clinical director, and to redefine management and first-line team leader responsibilities.

I worked with the management team as members designed an implementation plan for the restructured organization table and rewrote all four management-level job descriptions. Written and verbal presentations of structural changes and accompanying shifts in responsibilities were carefully mapped out before implementation. All first-line managers (with the title of Team Leader at this point in the consultation) were involved in the redesign of responsibilities affecting their positions.

Structural assessment, role redefinition, and introduction of changes were made within the first six months of the second consultation contract. Crucial to the success of the reorganization were the abilities of the agency director and the management team to be clear and consistent in their execution of newly defined responsibilities. Because there was a strong lack of confidence in the agency's leadership expressed during the assessment consultation, I prepared the management team for potential resistance to any changes that they would introduce to staff.

One of the central political issues that surfaced during the restructuring was a struggle for control within the agency. It was important for me to be cognizant of the political aspects of the changing agency, and to assist the management team in anticipating and responding to political side effects of the planning process (Craig, 1978). This struggle for control was evident both at the management level and between management and staff. As the management team began to institute new practices in problem areas, it was strongly challenged by line staff. Many staff did not believe that the administrative group could be making the changes and were convinced that I was doing all of the work. I encouraged the administrative group to demonstrate their own ideas and to include all levels of staff in the change process.

During the first year of implementation, the agency director and management team had to take considerable time to gather adequate information regarding problems, make informed decisions, communicate those decisions, and most importantly, not waffle at implementation. In the past, it was at implementation of a policy or practice that decisions were often reversed. This situation was often due to inadequate problem definition and goal setting. In the consultation effort it was important to sort out legitimate concerns and act upon them while not getting enmeshed in symbolic struggles. I was able to assist the management team by keeping focus on the clearly identified concerns raised during the assessment. Further, because a learning process was under way, it was impossible for the management team to make necessary changes without occasionally making mistakes. In part, it was a concern for pleasing all parties that had kept the management group paralyzed in the past. As an integral part of the consultation, potential outcomes and side effects were raised for consideration during the problem-solving process. In this way, proactive responses were increased.

My focus with the management team during this first six months of implementation had progressed from identifying with the team the key leadership issues that hindered them, redefining roles and responsibilities within their group and within the full agency structure, and then progressing to more specific problem areas. In this manner, the management team was able to tackle accountability and programmatic issues with increased trust and cooperation. The process, once established, became a cyclical problem-solving sequence in which the management team greatly increased its competence in responding to problems.

Management, clerical staff, and service delivery staff were affected by changes in practice. Each level had to be carefully included in the change process so that they could be successful in implementing new practices. All parties had to accommodate to change and get through resistance before they experienced any success. In meetings, I challenged the management team to consider new ways of responding and to adopt those strategies formally that seemed most effective. More reinforcing than my responses were the concrete improvements that began to accumulate.

Goal II involved the definition of ongoing functions and responsibilities of the agency governing board. This goal concerned the nature of the relationship between the board and the agency director.

Beginning in the first month of the consultation implementation, while I was working with the management team on their roles and leadership issues, I began to work with the governing board on definitions of the board's role in agency governance. This work required that I meet with the full board, officers, and committee chairs during evening hours, when they were most likely to be available. The board was eager to assist in the improvement of the agency, but was limited in the number of hours it could commit each month. As volunteers, the members of the board were generally unfamiliar with the complexity of the problems facing the agency.

One goal for me, then, was to increase the board's information base and, hopefully, the time commitment they could extend to the change process. I arranged as many consultation sessions as possible around monthly board meetings and executive committee meetings. The written consultation goal pertaining directly to board functions assisted me in keeping the groups on task. I was concerned that full understanding of the scope of the agency's problems might scare off board members. I arranged with the agency director and governing board officers that reports of progress on the consultation would be provided each month to the full board. These reports were integrated into the monthly board minutes.

The governing board worked with me in jointly reviewing committee functions, updating committee goals, establishing a long-range planning committee, and reviewing and expanding planning documents. What was more difficult to accomplish was the definition of the most effective role for the board.

The funding board wanted the agency governing board to take a more visible leadership role in setting agency direction. The governing board, however, was hesitant to take on increased responsibility. A major

consultation objective was jointly revised with the governing board's executive committee to include the redefinition of the board's role in regard
to support and tone (rather than direction) for the agency and its director.
This revision was critical in that it reemphasized the board's hesitance to
provide direction to the agency. Quite to my surprise, and the surprise of
the agency director, the governing board and director negotiated that the
director would take a stronger leadership position with the board, including chairing and convening board committees other than the executive
and finance committees.

Goal III concerned improvements in communication to be accomplished at all agency levels and between the agency, its board, the funder,
and referral sources. This goal affected not only the agency and its
governing board, but the administrative staff of the funding board. While
the consultation contract stated that funding administrators would be
involved in the consultation, the funders had no expectation that they
would have direct participation in the process.

Because the relationship with the funding board was critical to the
programmatic and economic survival of the agency, I determined that the
key funding administrators needed to be actively involved in improving
the lines of communication and in clarifying expectations with the agency.
In this regard, I was assuming a role of information expert (Lippitt &
Lippitt, 1986) as well as that of joint problem solver.

As work on this communication goal began, the funding administrators
and governing board officers seemed to want me to serve as their information conduit and interpreter to the other groups. I saw this as a trap to
my effectiveness. While I felt that I could assist the funding administrators
and governing board officers in clarifying their perspectives and expectations, I wanted them to communicate their thoughts directly with each
other. The issue of governing board versus funding board influence on the
agency was a critical one affecting the agency's future growth and independence. The agency would remain almost fully dependent upon the
funding board unless the governing board expanded its own role and
funding strategies.

I was challenged and often frustrated as I worked on this phase of the
consultation. When I talked independently with representatives of each
board, I found that each board wanted the other to provide clearer
direction to the agency and its director. Meanwhile, the director was trying
to take direction from both boards and was becoming confused in the
process. After gathering the perceptions of each group, I recommended a
series of meetings among the director, funding administrators, and agency

board officers. During these meetings the participants could explore the mutual expectations of the director and both boards and define less paternalistic funding board responses to the agency's crises. It took several rounds of encouragement to make these meetings happen.

In working with the communication issues, the funding board developed and implemented a new statement of philosophy and provided clarity to the agency regarding its new role. The funding board dramatically changed its relationship with its fundee agencies by giving each fundee agency responsibility for its own long-term economic survival. I played a more indirect role in these negotiations, encouraging the agency administrator and governing board to use their own improved lines of authority and communication in discussions with the funder. One side effect of the consultation was that the funding board administrators separately contracted with me for a few hours of consultation to assist them in defining roles and responsibilities within their own administrative group.

In considering improvements to accountability functions and communication, I encouraged agency management to identify systems for monitoring progress and for communicating with staff and outside groups. Once again, a task-focused and collaborative approach to the problem provided the structure for these changes. Some examples include the generation of monthly utilization rates for each staff member, a formal supervisory sequence to be used with staff experiencing performance problems, the strengthening of supervisory and monitoring functions of midmanagers, streamlined medical records procedures, the provision of more detailed reports to governing board committees, and an increase in the frequency of scheduled meetings throughout the agency. In each of these examples, the agency managers increased the amount and accuracy of information they provided to agency staff and governing board. They were able to keep their improvement plan on track and to reduce the number of unanticipated crises.

After approximately nine months of implementation, the management group and I decided that the agency administrators did not require my involvement at each of their meetings. The management team member in charge of clerical functions requested that I use some of the contracted consultation time to assist the clerical staff in their examination of clerical functions, work flow, and related job descriptions.

In a series of meetings over a three-month time span, the management team member, clerical staff, and I evaluated all of the clerical functions and work flow of the agency. I introduced and facilitated several structured information gathering steps to assist the clerical staff in the process.

These included conducting a time study of all clerical activities performed during a five-day period, identifying discrepancies in work load and job descriptions, reallocating resources for a smoother work flow, rewriting all job descriptions, and preparing desk manuals for each position. The clerical staff then instituted changes to improve tracking, billing, medical records, and auditing functions.

Year Two Implementation

At the end of the first year of implementation, the three central consultation goals had been realized. The agency administrators were not confident, however, that they could continue to practice the systems they had established without further consultative support. The agency contracted with me to provide two hours of weekly consultation during a second implementation year. The goals shifted to include monitoring and evaluating the management team's execution of their redefined roles, continuing to assist the governing board with the issue of leadership and direction, and further development of planning skills. I reduced the frequency of meetings with the whole management team and increased contact with the clinical program director and the program team leaders. The management team now operated more independently and only occasionally sought my assistance for monitoring their progress or reinforcement of a particular strategy we had designed.

During the second year of implementation, initial consultation efforts were concentrated on improving the working relationships between the clinical director and program team leaders. The program team leaders functioned as the mid-managers of the agency and reported directly to the clinical director. In spite of improvements to the structure of the program teams and reporting lines, the members of the mid-management group were unsure of the relationship between their responsibilities and their authority. In planning appropriate consultative interventions with this group, I felt that orienting the mid-managers and clinical director around similarities in their programs and responsibilities would both foster team development and provide the group with shared skills. My consultation remained collaborative and human-development focused, but additionally included more elements of the scientific-technological model. I still remained philosophically grounded in the educational and facilitative aspects of collaborative problem solving, but I determined that the agency would benefit from specific skill development in the area of planning. In this fashion, I began to serve as an expert provider of specific information, educator, and trainer (Gallessich, 1985; Kurpius & Brubaker, 1976; Rapin, 1989).

Several formal program planning efforts were undertaken. One example involved the design of a new case management plan. In using the same program development model I had previously introduced to the management team, the clinical director and program directors were able to extend their planning skills. The group found the formal aspects of planning to be cumbersome and foreign, and expressed that one round of training was insufficient to really cement the planning skills. The program directors, clinical director, and I served again as the core planning team, while using the program staff and central management team to help flesh out and review the plan. The resulting case management plan was endorsed so positively by the funding board that it was used as a model plan for other agencies.

In this more didactic interaction with the agency, it was important for me to remain collaborative in the execution of the planning process. I resisted requests to do the planning for the clinical director and program directors and worked with them to increase their own skill levels. In addition, I maintained the indirect consultative relationship with the direct line staff, working with the mid-management team as they included program staff in the planning process.

Midway through the second year, I was contracted for an additional four hours per week to provide consultation in the area of supervision. The assignment was consistent with my formal training as a counseling psychologist and educator. This consultation was designed as a one-year training experience in supervision for a program director who was seeking licensure as a psychologist. In this very specific consultation, I combined aspects of the human-development and scientific-technological models of consultation because I was both promoting development of a program director and staff while imparting specific supervisory knowledge and techniques. This consultation effort served as a model that the agency subsequently used with other outside supervisors.

At the conclusion of the second year of implementation, there was ample evidence that the central managers and program directors were executing their functions with increased skill and confidence. I was working with more developmental rather than remedial aspects of the agency and had almost eliminated meetings with the central administrative team. The management team and I were moving toward termination and establishing supports for the continuity of their improved practices (Lippitt & Lippitt, 1986). With each stage of the consultation agency managers seemed to

internalize the cyclical nature of the problem-solving process. While numerous challenges still faced the agency, each group with which I worked
was more able to generate solutions to problems and to accept responsibility for their actions.

Years Three and Four of Implementation

The consultation was extended for a third year, with my time devoted
to the training supervision already under way, the continuation of consultation on planning, and in providing consultation to the clinical director
and program directors on issues of supervision. During the first six months
of the year I spent approximately six hours per week in the agency, with
four hours devoted to the training supervision and two hours split between
planning and supervision topics. At the conclusion of the supervision
training consultation, I continued with the other two consultation components. This same relationship continued for six months of a fourth year of
implementation.

Consultation continued in the area of program planning but emphasized
the evaluative part of the planning process. I consulted with the clinical
and program directors as they implemented major program evaluation
efforts and two new program areas. The group was increasingly able to
generate planning questions, design implementation plans, and conduct
formal evaluations. I served as technical consultant and facilitator of their
process, demonstrating both human-development and scientific-technological consultation models. The clinical director and program directors
had acquired skills in program development and evaluation that would
assist them in problem solving, troubleshooting, and maintenance of the
agency's programs.

Because I was no longer regularly working with the top management
team, I monitored progress and potential trouble spots through my work
with one senior manager (the clinical director) and program directors, and
through informal contacts with the director and management team. Some
confusion about leadership of the agency, role definitions of key management team members, information flow among management layers, and
communication began to resurface with the program director and clinical
director group.

I encouraged the group to clarify these issues at their own level and to
use their planning skills to develop more satisfactory responses. In many
cases, the group was able to do so. Some of the concerns, however, involved central management. In these cases, I encouraged the group, and

particularly the clinical director, to bring the issues before the management team for their attention.

The re-emergence of some of the initial concerns identified during the assessment contract reinforced the cyclical nature of the consultation process. As the agency experienced difficult growth periods, members of the central management team retreated into old patterns. While the staff and program directors had almost completely turned over during the nearly four-year consultation, the management team had remained essentially intact. Administrative responses had improved greatly but required ongoing maintenance. My sense was that the management team was so relieved to be out of danger as an organization that they became lax in employing the evaluative checks we had designed earlier in the consultation. Leadership style and follow-through in the implementation of decisions were such impactful concerns at the onset of consultation that they required ongoing attention. The agency's consistent improvement in meeting its fiscal and performance expectations was testament to management's capacity to "recenter" again at the conclusion of the consultation.

Contract Completion

As I prepared to conclude the consultation approximately four years after my first contact, I interviewed the agency director about the consultation process. This activity provided us with the opportunity to celebrate the progress that the agency had made and allowed for the director to reflect on his experience throughout the process.

Evaluation

The original recommendations for action generated during the assessment consultation were converted to the goal-oriented plan for implementation. The detailed plan, which specified goals, objectives, and strategies in three critical areas of concern, served not only to guide my consultation during implementation, but also to frame the evaluation.

Progress was measured on every point of the plan, and presented to both the agency governing board and funding board. Because each level of the plan was tied to specific, documentable behaviors or written documents, progress was measured straightforwardly against the plan. Positive changes were implemented in all areas.

In the goal concerning the governing board's relationship to the director, the original goal was restructured dramatically. Rather than clarifying and strengthening the leadership functions of the governing board, the board decided finally to have the director take a more public role in the governance of the board. While the governing board seemed satisfied with this redefinition, I felt that it could have a long-term negative effect on the agency because it depended upon the leadership of one individual, the director.

After key components had been implemented, several evaluative measures were used to keep the plan on track. Management and mid-management job descriptions were reviewed for fit after six months of implementation and again in the second year of consultation. Slight modifications were made in some job descriptions and major changes were made in other positions to reflect increased job responsibilities. Internal audit functions were established to monitor progress on the fiscal and service delivery components of the agency.

While communication systems improved markedly in the first two years of consultation (increasing dialogue at all levels, improving information flow and information systems), long-term success in this area depended on consistency of action among all levels of the organization. In particular, those in the agency who held major leadership or linking positions were most apt to influence the lasting quality of communication.

As I consulted in the area of program development and evaluation, I considered the effects of the planners' program efforts to be the most realistic evaluation of my efforts. The agency managers were able successfully to design and implement a variety of new interventions and two entirely new service delivery areas. One of these was funded by a three-year Federal grant. In applying program evaluation skills, the agency was still struggling with data management, but had successfully maintained or expanded its programs with the aid of evaluation studies.

Evaluation: Reflections of the Agency Director

At the conclusion of the consultation, I conducted an exit interview with the agency director. I recorded the three-hour interview and include here excerpts that reflect the director's (XY) observations about the process of consultation, the consultant role and relationship, and consultee learnings and recommendations.

Process of Consultation

LR: You were trying to figure out, as you thought about the consultation, what was going wrong.

XY: Right.

LR: That you felt really overwhelmed at that time, not sure what was happening.

XY: Yeah, and I guess I was looking for, you know, I don't really know what I was looking for. I guess I was looking for something very concrete, that I could hang my hat on. A real quick fix remedy type of a thing.

LR: Um hm. Hoping for that?

XY: Yeah, I think so. And I guess at that point I really hadn't looked any farther than myself. I guess even subconsciously I was just assuming that it was all my fault and so we'll fix it real quick. Not really looking at the fact that there is a whole management structure in the agency, as well as the board and the agency's relationship with the funding board, you know, all the various nuances that exist there.

LR: Did you feel that before I came in and did the assessment, that focus on yourself?

XY: Oh yeah.

LR: So what happened for you when the data came back and there was so much loaded?

XY: Oh, I think it just reinforced it, that it was basically my problem. But as I said, you know, I kind of sifted through that after a while, and once I made the decision, to stick around and fight, it was almost kind of an energizing period. It's funny. Through the whole process I thought about quitting, but I never felt I was going to lose my job over it. I don't know why, when I look back in retrospect. Now maybe a lot of that was, you know, the support I felt from you. I think you were very up front in the beginning that we go this route, that this isn't going to be a lynch party.

LR: Right, absolutely.

XY: So that, in and of itself, may have given me some notion that I wasn't headed for the chopping block. If everybody was willing to put the time and money and the effort into this.

LR: Well, it sounds like that whole transition of looking at yourself as the pivotal person really responsible for the problems was one of the critical incidents, maybe the pivotal incident.

XY: Yes.

LR: Can you think, during that process of four years, whatever it was, of other critical times during the consultation? Either phases or particular aspects of the consultation that stand out for you?

XY: I don't think I was aware of how this whole thing was going to impact other management staff in the agency, and what a toll it was taking. Some of our meetings, I think, were so emotional. And I don't think I really expected or was aware of how this was affecting everybody.

LR: Um hm.

XY: That has helped, I think, considerably. What we went through and what we all shared made us much stronger as a group.

LR: Your ability to cope with problems and difficulties.

XY: Yeah, and I think a better ability to confront each other and to deal with things. I think we all use pretty much the same term every once in a while. You know, look, we've all been through so much in the past. We need to be up front with this.

LR: When you ask yourself those questions, when you tap your fingers and reflect, what do you end up answering?

XY: That things are OK. Oh, I mean I can always think of two or three issues that need to be dealt with, you know. But overall the agency's fine.

LR: The overall health is greatly improved.

XY: Oh yes. And I'm sure there will always be two or three issues that should be, that we should be dealing with. A lot of it is still doing a juggling act, prioritizing.

Consultant Role and Relationship

LR: Do you remember what you thought when we met, when it looked like I might end up being the person?

XY: Like I said, I felt very comfortable with you from the very beginning. I think I was pleased. I guess in my own mind I was expecting to get hooked up with some real aggressive somebody who thought they knew everything, who thought they were going to take care of everything real quick.

LR: What did you get instead?

XY: Somebody who obviously knew what she was doing, was not into quick fix remedies. Someone very supportive, and very honest as well. You know, I think one of the things I admired is, because I noticed a lot of times it was as tough on you as it was on us, was the fact that you could push, and you would push, and you would confront. Something else good about your style, about how you work, is I always felt that you tried to prepare me for what was coming. I never felt that anything was sprung on me.

LR: Good, I'm pleased to hear that.

These last questions have to do with our relationship, working together. Things that you see that might be helpful for people to know about the process. And any responses you had to me as an individual that might be important to reflect upon.

XY: Yeah, I thought about that a lot. Even from the very beginning, I had a great deal of trust in you. I can't really think of any major reasons why from the very beginning. Well, outside of the one about being up front about people's expectations whether I was going to get the axe or whatever. And I think that can be tough for a director or somebody in my position to trust somebody from the outside.

LR: What enabled you, can you tease out what enabled you to do that?

XY: I really don't know. I thought about that a lot. But I was instantly comfortable with you, from the first time I met you, which was down at the funding board.

LR: I remember that, um hm. Because you had considered several people.

XY: Oh, yeah, before they jumped on the bandwagon down there, I had talked to a couple people about doing it. As far as your style, your consultation style, I think for the most part I felt that you were almost a partner. You know.

LR: Was I good or bad?

XY: Good. I don't think you came in, or at least I never felt you were coming in from the standpoint "Well, here I am, the person with all the answers. Now I'm going to tell you what you need to do. And if you just do what I tell you to do then everything is going to be fine." You always let us make our own decisions. I never felt threatened by you, or felt that you were. That was never one of my concerns. Although I think you made it very clear from the front. I think you did a real good job with role clarification. If anything, I think you did a real good job of supporting the roles, our roles, and our responsibilities in the agency.

LR: That's nice to hear, because that's what I was picturing in my own mind, that might be helpful. To let each person find their own place, and not to assume that they shouldn't be there.

XY: I mean, I think you forced us to look at some painful issues sometimes. I'm surprised. I'm sure at some times you felt we needed a baseball bat to get us to deal individually or as a group with some issues.

LR: Yeah, I remember some really rough meetings. Leaving exactly as you described, you know. Could I crawl to the car? (both laugh) Did I have it in me to make it?

     How about the transition from the agency focus to what I've been doing for the last year or so, which has been kind of really redefined in terms of almost no contact with management staff except just casual things.

XY: I felt good about it. I guess you get to a point where I guess I felt like I
      wanted to move ahead.

      And I certainly was not threatened that you would be taking my manage-
      ment staff away. But I think a lot of that has to do with the fact that I think
      you did support the roles, and my role, my responsibility.

      I think the other thing too, and I again, maybe that's your approach, or
      your style. I think you never, you never let us feel that it was hopeless. The
      message was always there that you've got what it takes to do it. You may
      not want to do it, but you can. And I think that's important. I would certainly
      encourage anyone to go through the process. Once everything is all over
      and done with and you start looking around. It doesn't just stop with your
      management staff. It just has a ripple effect all the way down. I mean there
      are going to be certain things that are uncovered that you know that you
      are going to have to face.

Consultee Learnings and Recommendations

LR: I was just kind of reviewing the questions. I had the next item about any
      effects on the system.

XY: Well I think that is probably an effect right there. That for the first time, at
      least to my knowledge, that when an agency has experienced some problem
      the solution wasn't just to go and clean house. You know, instead of taking
      a look at what is going on and trying to fix it, to try to work with the existing
      agency personnel and staff. So I think that's probably a system effect or
      system impact. I think that the growth in the agency is indicative of the fact
      that, as far as the funding board is concerned, that we have our act together.
      I think it's a gesture of competence.

LR: Let's see. Here's a large subject which you have referred to in your earlier
      responses, in terms of things you have learned during the process as the
      director of the agency.

XY: I'd like to think I've learned how to motivate people, how to manage better.
      I learned a lot about myself. Just the statement I made before. That peoples'
      perceptions are real, was an important lesson for me.

LR: OK, you were saying that you learned how to manage and motivate people
      in a better way, a more effective way. Can you describe how that is?

XY: I think with being clearer myself on what I want and what I want to see,
      being able to communicate that to people. You can't really blame people for
      screwing up or not getting something done if you weren't clear at the
      beginning what you wanted. And I think, being as critical as I am of the

funding administrator about being sufficiently vague, I think there were times when I was just as vague. Just as indecisive, so I think I have become much more decisive, much more clear of what my expectations are. And certainly as a group, as an agency, we have certainly come a long way from functioning in a reactive pattern to much more proactive.

LR: That's one of the pieces that just seems to jump out at me.

XY: I mean, we will never be able to anticipate everything but I think we have just done a real 180 degree turn.

LR: If you were to give counsel to agencies considering such a process, be it agencies like this one or agencies in general, are there things that you feel would be helpful for them? Words of wisdom?

XY: Yeah. Don't go in with any preconceived ideas. Toughen yourself up. And be very involved from the very beginning. I remember being aggravated when it came time to write the actual goals for the consultation process because I was the one that was writing them, and I felt if I can write the goddam goals, then I ought to be able to figure out what the hell is wrong with this agency. But I think looking back, as far as hindsight is concerned, it was probably very important.

LR: You really got a chance to define your own destiny.

XY: Yeah, that I simply didn't sit back and let somebody else try to figure out, hopefully, what was to be accomplished during the course of this process. I think the other thing I would caution people on is to expect the unexpected. You know, when I look at my relationship with the agency board, I would not, maybe two, maybe three years ago, would not have expected that I would be basically not only running an agency but running a board of trustees.

LR: You know one thing that I think is delightful is that you feel able to talk about it.

XY: I learned well from it. God knows, I probably wasn't the first and won't be the last person who is in the position like mine, to have an opportunity to have an experience like this.

Interview Impact

Although I had reflected personally on the consultation and had used concrete progress in the structure and programs of the agency to guide my evaluation, I was greatly impressed by the reflections of the agency director. His great personal commitment to the consultation process served as a model for other levels of management participation.

Personal Learnings and Considerations for Training

The critical human development elements outlined by Conyne and O'Neil in Chapter 1 were reflected throughout the course of the four-year consultation. In working with various levels of the agency system, I used cyclical problem-solving processes to support the organization as it developed more effective management practices. While the agency was far healthier and more complex at the conclusion of the consultation, it can remain healthy only if its members continue to problem solve consistently and keep lines of communication open.

The consultation process began with a careful assessment of the organization. Assessment and interviewing skills were essential in my gaining the original consultation contract. My presentation of the long-term, developmental consultation approach as a recommended strategy aided the agency in committing to the consultation process. Negotiating ground rules during the initial contract meetings helped me greatly in establishing a trusting working relationship. Further, I was careful to operate within the data I was given.

My assessment design required familiarity with data-based strategies and instruments. Content analysis skills were used to organize the assessment results into naturally emerging themes. During the assessment stage, it was imperative that I not impose any particular set of assumptions about the source of the agency's problems. Future consultants need firm grounding in interview techniques and synthesizing models.

When the consultation moved from assessment to implementation, I formed a planning group to convert the assessment results to a written implementation plan. This collaboration helped me in developing a sound working relationship with the agency director and governing board and provided a framework by which both the agency and I could evaluate our progress. At each stage of the consultation I negotiated with the relevant consultee groups which problems were to be addressed, where to start, and how we would most effectively proceed in the problem-solving process.

While the specific problems changed over time, the basic intervention model remained the same. I kept a task focus and encouraged the members of the organization to look at ways they could increase their role effectiveness and problem solving skills. I had to be constantly mindful that I was not one of "them," that I was always an outside resource somewhat removed from the emotional life of the agency.

Much of the basic work of the consultation required that I have a good conceptual picture of the entire organization. It would not have been sufficient for me to respond to the interpersonal dynamics of the agency without also attending to systemic aspects of the organization. Redesigning the management structure, rewriting job descriptions, and modifying work flow patterns, for example, all required that I see the organization as a whole. Consultants in training need to be well grounded on the structure and developmental stages of organizations to be effective in intervening in complex organizations. Training in the specific skills of writing job descriptions, job redesign, and role enhancement would assist consultants in responding to the structural aspects of organizations. Many times communication problems are exacerbated by outdated structures.

The agency management was the identified consultee throughout the process, while I worked with several levels of managers. I worked with top levels of management first and then moved down in the management structure. Consultation trainees and practitioners often enter organizations where they may need to work with several organizational levels.

Almost every consultation intervention involved a group and required facilitation skills. Group skills training and supervised experience in group facilitation are natural core ingredients for aspiring consultants. Often, training programs do not give sufficient attention to this skill development area. Both knowledge of group process and practice in structured and unstructured group facilitation would enhance trainees' skill bases.

As the consultation progressed, fewer remedial and more proactive interventions were possible. Because of my training and experience, I was able to assist the agency in the areas of program development and evaluation. Thorough grounding in these content areas would aid developing consultants. Such training not only can provide a consultant with functional models to guide practice, but also can assist consultees in conceptualizing problems and solutions in positive and effective ways.

Personal values of independence, diversity, and collaboration are reflected in my consultation practice. Undertaking consultation as a major professional activity is often lonely and more unpredictable than other more traditional aspects of psychology practice. I have found that the consultation process is extremely rewarding and often intense. Consultants in training can anticipate dealing with high affect as they work with complex organizations.

Seeing organizations grow with my assistance is a great professional satisfaction. While long-term interventions allow for the development of rich working relationships and enduring system change, they do not fulfill the collegial need of talking with others who share similar work. It is important to develop support networks with other consultation professionals, not only to help broaden consultation skills but to gain emotional support for often difficult and challenging consultation assignments. I have yet to find a satisfactory answer to this dilemma. Pairing with other consultants, using a mentor system, participating in consultant support networks, seeking case consultations, and documenting consultation cases are possible supports for practicing consultants. Incorporating these elements, as well as close supervision, into the consultation training process would aid future consultants.

As I encouraged the members of the consultee agency to document their progress, I found that keeping notes on the progress of the consultation was very helpful to me. Not only was I able to keep myself and the consultees on track with the aid of my ongoing records, but I was able to look back and see concrete progress that I had made with the agency. Documenting the process through the writing of this chapter has been an invaluable learning tool, as well.

Trainees, then, can consider a number of potential core training components and additional training areas that might give them desirable expertise. Interviewing skills, knowledge and practice in a variety of assessment techniques, broad knowledge of how organizations work, group facilitation skills, program development and evaluation techniques, and knowledge of models of consultation were key to the case I have presented. Skill development in data management, supervision, personnel management, and knowledge about a particular type of consultee organization are examples of additional consultant skill areas that trainees might pursue. Specializing in a type of intervention or a type of organization can give a consultant focused skill and experience.

References

Conyne, R., & O'Neil, J. (1990, August). *A context for organizational consultation* [Paper part of the symposium, Organizational Consultation in Counseling Psychology—four case studies: Training implications]. Paper presented at the annual meeting of the American Psychological Association, Boston.

Craig, D. (1978). *Hip pocket guide to planning and evaluation.* Austin, TX: Learning Concepts.

Gallessich, J. (1985). Toward a meta-theory of consultation. In D. Brown & D. Kurpius (Eds.), Consultation [Special issue], *The Counseling Psychologist, 13,* 336-354.

Insel, P., & Moos, R. (1974). *Work Environment Scale, Form R.* Palo Alto, CA: Consulting Psychologists Press.

Kurpius, D., & Brubaker, J. (1976). *Psychoeducational consultation: Definitions—functions—preparation.* Bloomington: Indiana University Press.

Lippitt, G., & Lippitt, R. (1986). *The consulting process in action* (2nd ed.). La Jolla, CA: University Associates.

Moore, M., & Delworth, U. (1976). *Training manual for student service program development.* Boulder, CO: Western Interstate Commission for Higher Education.

Rapin, L. (1989, March). *Human services consultation: Implications for counselor education.* Paper presented at the annual meeting of the American Association for Counseling and Development, Boston.

Robinson, S., & Gross, D. (1985). Ethics of consultation: The Canterville ghost. *The Counseling Psychologist, 13,* 444-465.

Schein, E. (1969). *Process consultation: Its role in organization development.* Reading, MA: Addison-Wesley.

Schein, E. (1987). *Process consultation: Lessons for managers and consultants* (Vol. 2). Reading, MA: Addison-Wesley.

Walton, R., & Warwick, D. (1973). The ethics of organization development. *Journal of Applied Behavioral Science, 2,* 681-698.

3

Implementing School-Based Consultation Services: An Analysis of Five Years of Practice

JOSEPH E. ZINS

THIS chapter examines essential issues in the development of a consultation-based, psychological services delivery program through discussion of the five years of experiences I had within an educational organization. It also includes commentary on the central consultation concepts identified by Conyne and O'Neil in Chapter 1, along with illustrations of many of these points. Recollections of my conversations with key participants in the consultation program are reported, as are my personal reactions to the experiences. The primary goal is to describe the processes that occurred as I implemented the consultation program and brought about organizational change, neither of which is usually reported in most case studies (e.g., Lippitt, Langseth, & Mossop, 1985). A final intent is to encourage adoption of alternative educational delivery systems (see Graden, Zins, & Curtis, 1988).

School-based consultation is defined as "an indirect method of providing preventively-oriented psychological (or educational) services in which

AUTHOR'S NOTE: I wish to acknowledge the contributions of the numerous persons who collaborated in the development of the psychological services program described in this chapter. In addition, the support and encouragement of Charlene R. Ponti is greatly appreciated.

consultants and consultees engage in a cooperative problem solving process to enhance students' well-being and performance" (Zins & Ponti, 1990b, p. 206). Participants jointly work to identify problems and develop solutions rather than having the psychologist take responsibility for the case as is done in traditional clinical approaches. Involving consultees in the problem-solving process may take more time, but it also capitalizes on the expertise of all parties, encourages creativity, increases consultee involvement, and can lead to better understanding of student-related problems and to improved consultee skills that can be applied in the future. The approach is similar to the "human-development" system of consultation proposed by Gallessich (1985), although I also relied upon what she referred to as "social/political" and "scientific-technological" systems in specific situations.

Within this model, consultation is used as the overarching framework to deliver all other psychological services. That is, all requests for assistance from the psychologist begin with a consultative problem identification interview that emphasizes selection of a target behavior and involves baseline data collection procedures (see Figure 3.1) (Kratochwill & Bergan, 1990; Zins & Ponti, 1990a). The assessment activities listed in Figure 3.1 (e.g., classroom behavioral observations) serve the purposes of (a) gathering additional data to clarify the problem to supplement information provided by the consultee, and/or (b) establishing a baseline. Once the problem is defined and baseline data collected, problem analysis occurs as shown. Next, potential solutions such as classroom interventions, counseling, or a referral to an outside agency are generated, with one then selected for implementation to resolve the problem situation. Finally, the outcomes of the chosen intervention are monitored and evaluated through data-based means. From this perspective, the majority of psychological services provided in schools are indirect rather than direct (Gutkin & Conoley, 1990).

As a final point of introduction, readers are reminded that the case represents a retrospective analysis of what happened as I worked as a school consultant. Consequently, although I spent considerable energy examining the consultation process at that time, explicit identification and clarification of some concepts and issues occurred to me after my relationship with the district was terminated. Further, although an actual case is reported, much descriptive information has been altered to disguise the identities of the parties involved.

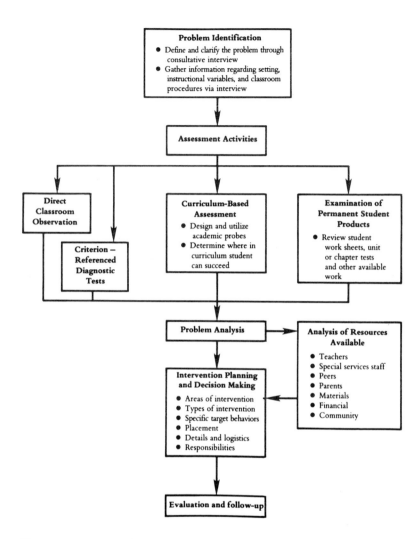

Figure 3.1. Flow Chart for Problem Identification and Intervention Planning Interviews

SOURCE: Based on Lentz, 1987. Reprinted from Zins, Curtis, Graden, and Ponti (1988), *Helping Students Succeed in the Regular Classroom.* Copyright © 1988, Jossey-Bass Publishers, Inc., San Francisco. Reprinted by permission.

Setting and Background Issues

Setting

The setting for the case was the Westmont Public Schools, a suburban district of approximately 2,100 students. During the years reviewed, I served as the system's psychologist, on a contractual basis through the local community mental health center (CMHC) for the first two years, and as one of its employees during the later three years. Dr. Niehaus served as Superintendent, and he was supported by a Leadership Team consisting of Assistant Superintendents, principals, and assistant principals.

In addition to the regular education program, a full range of special education services were available, and classes for the academically gifted were instituted during the period of the study. Support personnel in addition to the psychologist included guidance counselors, special education teachers, teacher aides, speech and language therapists, and a school nurse.

Background Issues

The Westmont district had contracted with various professionals for a limited range of psychological services, primarily psychological evaluations, for perhaps 20 years prior to the time of the case study. Most recently, the CMHC had been the provider agency.

Several years before the beginning of the case, the district arranged a contract that included "consultation" services in addition to the usual psychological evaluations. According to what was related to me, these services in fact consisted of sensitivity training groups for teachers. Several faculty expressed strong reservations about these experiences, and the contract for "consultation" subsequently was not renewed. Around this same time, one principal became disenchanted with a psychologist who conducted the psychological evaluations of students for his school, and he shared these feelings with the Leadership Team. Thus some negative feelings about the psychological services program existed.

Public Law 94-142 (The Education of the Handicapped Act) was adopted by the federal government at about this time. Among its requirements, the law called for a free and appropriate public education for *all* children, and for multifactored, multidisciplinary assessments of children with suspected handicaps. However, the potential resource implications and specific requirements for schools were not yet clearly understood.

Due to the limited range and amount of psychological services provided, relatively few students were recipients of these services. Nevertheless, when I began working with the district, I realized that there was at least some interest in broadening the range of psychological services as indicated by its prior willingness to contract for the consultation/sensitivity training. At this point, however, the district was not actively seeking to expand or decrease the psychological services program.

Overview of the Consultation Plan and the Consultation Issues

To provide an overview of the case study, this section outlines the series of systematic and purposeful activities that occurred. The consultation plan gradually evolved as I became acquainted with district needs, began to provide consultation services, and refined my conceptualization of the psychological services delivery model.

In contrast to the other cases in the book, I was not called into the Westmont Schools to assist with specific organizational issues. Instead, the district requested a meeting with the CMHC to discuss renewal of the psychological services contract, and as a potential provider of the services, I was asked to participate in the negotiations. To contribute to the process, an initial task for me was to become familiar with the district's organization, operation, and philosophy, the previous services delivery system, and its perceived needs. Also crucial was to determine if my orientation was compatible with the needs and philosophy of the district, and whether I would be an appropriate person to assume responsibility for providing the services delineated in the contractual arrangement.

Efforts also had to be directed toward relationship building, particularly to overcome the resistances that had developed following the sensitivity training conducted by the earlier consultant. As it turned out, this took a long time. Additional objectives that eventually arose included making both individual and organizational consultation services available, fully developing consultation as an integral component of the educational services delivery system, and incorporating a preventive focus to enhance the probability of more extensive effects. In addition, attempts to improve the quality of all psychological services were initiated through introduction of accountability and program evaluation procedures.

During these activities, a number of consultation issues emerged that were essential to address in order to implement and operate the program effectively. These included: (a) assessing the organization's need for consultative services, (b) convincing the consultee system about the merits of consultation, (c) establishing an effective working relationship, (d) changing consumer expectations regarding the consultant's role and function, (e) developing consultation as an essential educational service, (f) implementing marketing strategies to ensure maximum utilization and accessibility of consultation, (g) documenting the effectiveness and outcomes of the service, and (h) determining an appropriate consultation ideological system. As will be evident in later discussions, some of these issues were particularly significant in this case, but generally all must be dealt with whenever consultation services are introduced (see Lippitt et al., 1985). They are discussed in greater detail in subsequent sections of the chapter.

Program Implementation

In this section the various steps through which the consultation program was introduced and implemented are reviewed in depth. Consistent with other chapters, the material is generally organized according to the phases suggested by Lippitt and Lippitt (1986). The discussion begins with initial entry and organizational assessment, proceeds to the point at which consultation became the foundation from which all other psychological services were delivered and the range of services expanded, and concludes with discussion of resistances encountered.

Entry and Relationship Establishment

Entry into the system was not a one-step occurrence. Rather, it consisted of a long series of carefully planned, systematic, and interrelated activities that took place over two to three years, designed to address the consultation issues mentioned earlier. Specific activities are discussed throughout the program implementation section of this chapter.

My entry into the district was initiated when a representative from the CMHC and I began meeting with a representative of the schools regarding renewal of the psychological services contract. During this time I made a special effort to model the collaborative problem-solving process, which is the cornerstone of the consultative approach. By demonstrating this relationship style, I hoped to reduce some of the negative feelings that existed. Further, the organizational change literature suggests that simply providing information is not sufficient in itself to change a system, but needs to be supplemented with other change efforts concurrently (Maher, Illback, & Zins, 1984). Modeling can be helpful in this respect.

Problem Identification Through Organizational Analysis

To prepare for meeting with the Assistant Superintendent and others involved in the contractual negotiations, I conducted an initial organizational assessment to gain a familiarity with the schools. Of particular interest were factors that might indicate support for the introduction of consultation services, as they would determine whether I was the most appropriate person to serve the district. Depending upon the outcome of the needs assessment, these data might demonstrate to decision makers that there was a need for more comprehensive psychological services that could lead to more effective and efficient organizational operation. If the consultative model was not appropriate, another psychologist most likely would provide the services.

As part of the organizational analysis, I met with several of my CMHC colleagues who had previous experience working with this district. They provided historical information regarding the CMHC's relationship with the schools, the specific terms of previous contractual agreements, and their personal recollections of working in the district. Ms. Bieili, a mental health therapist, was particularly helpful in this regard. She had counseled numerous students and families from the district as well as talked with many teachers over the years. A number of these students were experiencing significant behavioral problems, and Ms. Bielli reported that it was a challenge for teachers to meet their needs in the classroom. Her insight, understanding, and guidance proved invaluable to me, and these consultative interactions (in which we were both consultants and consultees) were the beginnings of our long-term, close collaboration.

In addition to discussions with colleagues, I reviewed year-end summary reports that the district published. I also read recent editions of the community magazine and spoke with professionals in community agencies (e.g., juvenile court, child protective services) regarding their perceptions of the district and its needs. Further, I already was knowledgeable about state and federal rules and regulations that might impact on the schools in general and upon the provision of consultation services in particular.

Through the data gathering process, I learned that the district was recognized as a leader in terms of providing high quality, innovative educational services. It had a philosophical orientation that promoted an open social climate, and it explicitly was committed to meeting the needs of individual students. At the time, it was one of the only districts in the state that had *any* type of regular psychological services. Further, I concluded that there potentially would be far greater needs for psychological services as Public Law 94-142 became operationalized due to its requirement that public schools serve all children within the least restrictive setting. Consultation would be a particularly important support service with respect to the increased demands associated with educating students with handicaps.

Through these discussions I also became aware of problems that I might face regarding the introduction of an expanded psychological services program. Because the perceptions of school personnel regarding professional roles are based in part upon past experiences (Gallessich, 1973), I anticipated that (a) extensive efforts would have to be put into relationship building, (b) consultation would have to be clearly defined and understood, and (c) school personnel most likely would perceive me initially as someone who provided "testing" services. I also learned that the district had a reputation for being fiscally conservative (e.g., they were involved in energy conservation before it became "fashionable").

In sum, my analysis to this point suggested that my interest in providing consultation services was consistent with the apparent needs of the district, although it would be necessary to establish trusting relationships, to cultivate these potential needs and increase the district's awareness of them, and to deal with misconceptions about consultation. The philosophical orientation and organizational climate appeared conducive to consultation (e.g., Kuehnel, 1975), and it seemed desirable to be able to demonstrate the beneficial nature of the services through accountability techniques.

Contractual Arrangements, Goal Setting, and Action Planning

Obtaining Administrative Acceptance

As mentioned earlier, the initial contractual meetings were conducted in the spring with one of the Assistant Superintendents. Our first formal discussions initially focused on continuation of the contract for conducting psychoeducational assessments. Once we agreed on this issue and I had developed a good relationship with the Assistant Superintendent, I introduced the idea that consultation services may help meet district needs. Consultation was described as an indirect, collaborative problem-solving process in which a consultant and consultee directed their joint efforts and expertise toward resolving work-related issues to benefit students. (Actually, the term *indirect* was never used in describing these services due to the possible negative connotations that it might have. Instead, the approach was presented as being a means of supporting teachers so that they could more effectively work with students.)

Among the aspects of consultation emphasized were that it was intended to (a) extend the expertise of the psychologist to more students, (b) focus on the prevention and early detection of problems, (c) empower consultees and enhance their skills, (d) utilize staff skills more efficiently and effectively, and (e) develop a broader range of positive alternatives for students. These same concepts were also used later when the approach was presented to teachers and parents. The additional support that would be available to teachers and administrators as Public Law 94-142 was implemented was also emphasized, as it was anticipated that these persons would experience increased responsibilities with regard to mainstreaming students with handicaps. Further, consultation was described as an essential aspect of psychoeducational assessment rather than as a relatively separate activity. Misconceptions about what consultation entailed also were addressed. The data I collected to support this change in orientation were shared, and I suggested engaging in additional needs assessment activities.

After numerous lengthy discussions, the Assistant Superintendent decided to support the idea of expanding the psychological services program, and we decided that the building principals and key faculty members should be approached with the proposal to further clarify interests and needs. First, I spoke with each principal. Once I gained their support and learned of their needs, I met with them again along with several representative faculty members, to discuss the proposal. Each time I went through a similar explanation about consultation as I had done with the Assistant Superintendent. Teachers also were supportive of the proposal, and agreed that there was a need for additional, broader services. They believed that the entire faculty likewise would be receptive.

Finally, Superintendent Niehaus was approached after he had discussed the issue with the Leadership Team. Again, the need for consultation services was described, the model was outlined, and his questions were answered. Although the Superintendent was cautious about agreeing to expand the psychological services program, he became more accepting when informed that I intended to conduct an end-of-year evaluation that would be shared with him as well as with the school board (if he so desired). He also was aware that the contractual agreement periodically would be reassessed. When finally approving the contract in which I would provide two hours of consultation services to each school each week (in addition to conducting psychological evaluations), Dr. Niehaus suggested that many of the administrators also might wish to avail themselves of the consultative services. To me, this statement indicated the depth of his support.

Following finalization of the contractual agreement, details of the consultation program still had to be worked out with each principal before formally introducing it to the faculty. Although I had briefly discussed many issues with them, I felt a need to review and reinforce issues such as confidentiality and the voluntary nature of consultation, as I believed these potentially could be problematic areas. The principals understood the necessity for teachers to feel that they could talk freely with me, but they also understandably needed to be aware of events occurring within their schools. Consequently, it was essential to build a trusting, open relationship. To facilitate this process, we agreed to follow the "need to know" principle. That is, if I became aware during consultation of something about which they should be aware, I would do my best to have the teacher and/or myself (with the teacher's permission) inform the principal of the matter. Obviously, such an arrangement called for significant trust on the part of the principals; nevertheless, each agreed to this arrangement, again with the understanding that we would review the services periodically. The collaborative approach was quite helpful in these delicate negotiations.

It was equally important to stress that teachers' participation had to be voluntary to obtain their maximum involvement. The principals were gently requested not to exert "pressure" on teachers to consult, while at the same time asked to encourage teachers to work with me and to provide whatever support they could for the consultation services program. In this particular case, the issue of voluntary participation was especially important to clarify because the district paid a high hourly rate to the CMHC for my services and thus did not wish to see me "idle." At the same time, I felt a strong need to become assimilated into the system quickly so that my services were utilized to the maximum extent.

Gaining Staff Acceptance

Following these extensive discussions, I met with the staff of each school during the first faculty meeting of the year to introduce myself and to inform them of the availability of the psychological services program. Use of an "entry presentation" such as this (Zins & Curtis, 1984) to explain consultation services is based upon evidence suggesting that organizations may be more receptive to the introduction of new programs that they understand than to those that they do not (Reimers, Wacker, & Koeppl, 1987).

These presentations were made in each school to the entire faculty, including the principal. Among the topics covered were the rationale, goals, and intended outcomes of consultation, an explanation of the consultative problem-solving process, confidentiality, a brief description of appropriate problems, and an explanation of logistical issues (i.e., when I'd be at the school, how to arrange an appointment) (see Zins & Illback, in press). I also emphasized that seeking assistance did not imply deficient skills. An audio-visual program was also presented on several occasions as another means of explaining the consultative problem-solving process. Again, I was as collaborative as possible in my interactions in order to model this relationship style. This process is reflective of the human-development ideological system of consultation (Gallessich, 1985).

Having the principals in attendance served several purposes. It demonstrated administrative support for the services, and it also enabled them to answer procedural questions. More importantly, their presence during the discussion of confidentially indicated that they understood and supported this aspect of consultation.

The major concerns expressed by teachers were what types of cases were appropriate to discuss, and what kinds of information should be brought to the sessions. Based upon the number of questions asked, the level of attention during my presentations, and the comments made, I perceived teachers to be supportive of the expanded services. The principals later confirmed my perceptions. Now I was eager to begin!

Taking Action and Cycling Feedback

Expanding the Services Provided

Once I entered the consultee system, I aggressively proceeded to make consultation available by being as accessible as possible to teachers, inter-

TABLE 3.1 Reported Usage of Consultation Services

	Percentages				
Category	Year I	Year II	Year III	Year IV	Year V
Faculty using services	78.1	94.3	93.7	94.5	94.0
Frequency of usage					
One time	34.3	6.1	0.0	2.7	3.1
Two-three times	37.5	30.6	28.2	23.1	15.5
Four or more times	28.2	63.2	71.8	(74.1)	(81.4)
Four-five times	*	*	*	28.6	23.3
Six or more times	*	*	*	45.5	58.1

NOTE: *These categories were not collected during Years I through III. The numbers in parentheses in Years IV and V are aggregates of usage frequencies one through four times, and are included to allow comparisons with Years I through III.

acting with them whenever I could even if it was not for consultation, and encouraging them to talk with me before problem situations became severe. The program quickly became accepted in each school and many teachers began to consult regarding the academic and behavioral problems their students experienced. Several special education teachers especially made use of the service. Satisfied teachers were very helpful in terms of promoting the program as they frequently encouraged their colleagues to consult with me whenever problems arose.

During the first year the contract specified that I consult one day per week in addition to conducting psychoeducational evaluations (with consultation provided in conjunction with the evaluations). After the first semester or so, however, it became apparent that more time for consultation was needed due to the heavy demands for services. I documented teachers' reported use of consultation (see Table 3.1) and the principals observed that many requests for assistance were made. At the end of the year a number of teachers also let the administration know that they desired to have additional consultative assistance available in the future. Thus the contract during Year II was expanded from approximately one to three days of psychological services per week. Not only was I working with teachers and administrators, but I also gradually began to consult with parents and occasionally provided individual counseling. In addition to my services, a contract with Ms. Bielli, the mental health therapist, was arranged in Year II enabling her to provide weekly group counseling in each school. Consultation was starting to become a widely accepted service.

Prior to Year III, Dr. Niehaus called me at home one Saturday and asked for my reaction to the possibility of working full-time for the district. He said that the principals and teachers were very satisfied with the services rendered, but strongly felt that there was a need to expand the quantity available (partially based on the data in Table 3.1 indicating that a large percentage of the teachers reported consulting with me). Being a responsible administrator, however, he was not certain whether there was enough work to warrant a full-time position. Therefore, if I were interested in the job, he would contact a small adjoining district to explore the possibility of my working there one day per week, and for Westmont the other four days. When I responded affirmatively and the adjoining district did likewise, I met with Dr. Niehaus. As we finalized our agreement for me to become a district employee, he made a comment similar to, "I don't want you to be like a lot of those psychologists who spend most of their time giving tests. You have many more skills to offer. We're hiring you to provide consultative assistance to our teachers, administrators, and parents." Needless to say, his support made my day and was an important consultation outcome. Further discussion of the transition from external to internal consultant is contained in the next section.

During this time I worked extensively with administrators as well as teachers. For this reason and because my office was in the central administration building, it was necessary to avoid being viewed by teachers as "one of them" (i.e., an administrator). Indeed, for that reason I requested that my name not be listed on district letterhead along with central office administrators, and I also asked these persons to be cautious of how they referred to me in conversations with teachers. Essentially, I did not want to be viewed as "belonging" to either group, even though this left me somewhat isolated professionally (which was one reason for establishing the professional peer support group described later). The danger in being associated primarily with one group was that I could become excluded or hindered in my work with the other group.

During Year III demand for services continued to increase (see Table 3.1). Teachers more frequently sought my assistance before problem situations became severe. I also was asked to participate in many Leadership Team meetings, and spent increasing time working with parents regarding problems their children were experiencing. Although it was satisfying to have the opportunity to work with so many teachers and parents as well as to consult at an organizational level, the need to expand the amount of services again surfaced. Consequently, the agreement to share my services with the adjoining district was discontinued after Year III, and I worked full time for Westmont during the last two years of the case study.

Transition From External to Internal Consultant

Although I greatly missed the opportunity to consult routinely with my CMHC colleagues, I did not experience a great deal of other change once I became a district employee. The most significant advantage was that I had more time to provide services and additional flexibility in determining how I directed my efforts. Because I already was very committed to helping the district achieve its goals, was widely accepted as a member of the school team, and levels of mutual trust were high, there were not noticeable changes in the staff's perceptions of me in these respects. However, due to our increased interactions, I recall becoming more understanding of teachers' responsibilities and of the pressures they faced, which probably helped me become a better consultant.

Although as a district staff member I occasionally felt that my perspectives on problem situations had become narrower than in the past, the primary disadvantage I experienced following my change to internal consultant status was the reduced opportunity to consult with other mental health professionals. I enjoyed my contacts with the interdisciplinary CMHC staff tremendously and often relied upon them to assist me with challenging issues. Partially in response to this issue, several psychology colleagues from other districts and I established a professional peer support group.

A peer support group is "a small group of professionals with a common area of interest who meet periodically to learn together and to support one another in their ongoing professional development" (Kirschenbaum & Glaser, 1978, p. 3). Each participant in our group faced similar challenges in attempting to develop a psychological services program because such services were new to our geographic area and our schools. Through this group, we were able to receive support and encouragement regarding our efforts, obtain concrete suggestions about practical issues, and solicit technical assistance for resolving problems that arose (Zins, Maher, Murphy, & Wess, 1988). We engaged in scientific-technological as well as human-development consultation (Gallessich, 1985) with one another. Among the learning formats used were presentation and review of cases, instruction by guest speakers and members, discussion of journal articles, and group problem solving. Participation in the group was found to be very helpful in terms of facilitating interactions with other colleagues and in preventing feelings of isolation and burnout. Most of us learned many ideas about intervention development through our meetings.

Integrating Consultation Into Organizational Routines

The entry process continued for several years as I promoted consultation as a routine component of the educational system and worked to expand the number of persons who utilized the service. Each year I attended the first faculty meeting at each school to remind teachers of the availability of consultation services and to deal with their suggestions and concerns. I also was on the orientation session agendas for new teachers to explain my role. Once school began and the new teachers were settled, I met with them individually to clarify more fully my role and the consultation process. In addition, I spoke to student teachers assigned to the district to familiarize them with my services. Although few of them ever worked with me, my efforts were intended to help these future teachers develop a better understanding of the psychologist's role, and to inform them of the availability of this potential resource.

Periodic formative reviews of the psychological services program were held, most often during Years I and II, to ensure district satisfaction and to make any necessary modifications. While no major changes were necessary, the meetings promoted an atmosphere of open communication and trust.

As mentioned earlier, an interesting development was that administrators started consulting with me frequently. I made specific efforts to develop good relationships with them and to inform them of my availability for consultation. Those who began working with me shared their positive reactions with the Leadership Team. As they made more use of my services, these sessions often consumed significant portions of my time each week. Topics addressed included personnel issues, school and district-wide policies, development of a program for the academically gifted, curricular changes, and coordination of efforts with outside agencies. I also became quite active in the operation of the special education program, often using a scientific-technological consultation system, because I had a relatively extensive knowledge of Public Law 94-142 procedures.

The following illustrates how the psychological services program became a routine aspect of the educational system. At one school a teacher, special services staff member, and I (among others) noted that a number of students had social skills difficulties. After discussing our observations, the three of us decided, with the principal's approval, to set up short-term, kill-oriented social skills groups. Very specific goals were established and activities were derived from various published curricula, and six or seven students participated in each group. The teacher and special services provider, who both had prior experience/training with such activities, led the groups and I consulted regularly with them.

Another significant occurrence was that over the years an expansion occurred in the conceptualization of consultation services. When consultation initially was introduced, it was somewhat distinct from assessment, counseling, and so forth, even though I tried to integrate these activities. This distinction was necessary at first in order to have consultation gradually accepted. However, there slowly was a change so that an overall "consultative framework" for psychological services emerged. Thus all psychological services began to be provided through the consultation process. Assessment, for example, was seen as a means of problem identification (see Figure 3.1). Administering standardized tests or conducting behavioral observations were merely ways of clarifying problems that led to intervention development. Or, counseling was viewed as an intervention resulting from consultation. Once psychological services were conceptualized in this manner, services delivery seemed to become more efficient and better integrated. In fact, a policy eventually was adopted that stipulated that three interventions were to be attempted and their outcomes documented *before* a multifactored assessment was conducted, which certainly encouraged consultation. In cases in which these interventions were ineffective, we had far better ideas about the assessment questions that needed to be answered, and assessment became a means of developing interventions rather than only a method of diagnosis or classification.

Teachers and parents also began routinely to seek consultation directly for assistance, and rarely referred students for psychoeducational evaluations in order to request help (as is often done in many districts). Although contemporary procedures such as "prereferral intervention" and "intervention assistance" (see Zins, Curtis, Graden, & Ponti, 1988) had not been conceptualized, the consultation system in the Westmont Schools clearly was a forerunner to these practices.

We also established regular meetings at the middle/high school to coordinate the services offered by the psychologist, the counselors, and the nurse, with one of the assistant principals often attending. Our goal was to facilitate our individual efforts with students as they progressed through the school. The nurse and I both worked with all grade levels and thus were able to provide a longitudinal perspective. The counselors organized their duties so that they were responsible for students in specific grades; thus, those in charge of the earlier grades served as resources to their colleagues. These weekly meetings were very productive in developing practical strategies for assisting students, resulted in more coordinated efforts, and were an efficient use of resources.

As requests for services increased each year, it became apparent that there were far more needs in the district than I would ever be able to meet by myself. Again, the data in Table 3.1 documents my extensive involvement. Therefore, I proposed that the learning disability teachers expand their roles to provide consultative assistance, too, particularly with regard to academic problems, to meet the demand.

There were two primary obstacles to overcome for this change to occur. First, none of the teachers had training in consultation, and we knew that there was preliminary evidence that low-skilled consultants may have a detrimental effect on consultation outcomes (Curtis & Watson, 1980). Second, if the teachers engaged in such activities on a regular basis, the amount of time for direct instruction would decrease. On the other hand, they already routinely assisted regular education teachers on an informal basis before and after school, at lunch time, and so forth. The district concluded that even though there would be a slight decrease in direct instruction in the learning disability program, more students actually would benefit from the expertise of these teachers. Further, because there clearly was a need for additional support services and the administration acknowledged the importance of formal training, I was asked to conduct a consultation training program during Year IV for the learning disability teachers. Following the training, these teachers negotiated with their principals to set aside time to consult. The district level administration supported these services but wanted principals to decide whether it was feasible within individual schools. Most principals and teachers worked out an arrangement, but teachers who did not continued to consult on a less formal and regular basis as they had in the past, hopefully using more effective techniques.

One additional point about integrating consultation into organizational routines merits mention. When I became a school employee in Year III, I was asked to draft a job description because none existed. In it consultation was listed prominently as a major responsibility. Because it was explicitly delineated in the job description approved by the administration, consultation now became an officially sanctioned activity.

Marketing Strategies Directed to Expand Consumer Groups

Both low- and high-intensity approaches were used to market the psychological services program to various consumer groups (Rothman, Teresa, Kay, & Morningstar, 1983). Low-intensity efforts are those that tend to be impersonal and inexpensive, while high-intensity ones use a more personal approach and therefore are more costly.

Low-intensity approaches included announcements and information about the program in school, PTA, and community newsletters, notices in the Superintendent's Monday Morning Bulletin, and other written descriptions distributed to teachers regarding the availability of the services. Even the student yearbook was useful in increasing my visibility. During my first year as a district employee, several yearbook staff members wanted to include a picture of me testing a student. Although I welcomed the exposure that I would receive, I suggested instead that they depict me consulting with teachers. What finally appeared was my individual photo along with another larger one in which I was consulting with three counselors, as we actually did each week. The story accompanying the pictures read, " 'We care about the emotional as well as the academic development of the students,' said Dr. Joseph Zins . . . who spent time each week consulting with counselors, principals, and teachers, and discussing problems in students' behavior or academic achievements." The caption on the larger picture of me and the counselors stated, "Mr. Dan Sutton, Dr. Joseph Zins, Miss Virginia Bell, and Mrs. Victoria Bluestone meet each week to discuss ways they can help students." Great publicity!

Most of the marketing efforts, however, involved high-intensity efforts. I frequently spoke at PTA meetings, was on the agenda at orientation sessions, gave presentations at the first faculty meeting at each school yearly, participated in district-wide curriculum development, and became involved in community-based activities such as a substance abuse prevention program. At one point I was even asked to give a talk (actually described as a "sermon") at one of the local churches as they thought I could provide valuable insight from a psychological perspective on one of the commandments. (It was quite an experience to drive up to the church on Sunday morning and see my name on the marquee. I had spoken at national professional conferences in the past, but this experience was *exceedingly* more anxiety provoking for me—I couldn't sleep the night before for one of the only times in my entire life—and it tested the limits of how far I was willing to go with respect to marketing my services!) A few additional examples of high-intensity marketing activities follow.

I developed a good working relationship with a high school social sciences teacher (and in fact, I believe she was influenced to pursue her Ph.D. in psychology partially as a result of our interactions) and served as a guest lecturer in her classes each year. My goals were to present topical information, to familiarize students with the services I provided, and to expose them to psychology as a career option. A similar arrangement existed with the home economics teacher when her classes covered family life education and substance abuse. As a result of these talks, students viewed me as another potential resource. In fact a number of them made appointments to see me after these sessions, and in several instances students later asked me to intervene when their friends made suicidal threats. I believe that these calls were motivated in part by these talks.

In my final year the Assistant Superintendent in charge of staff development approached me to discuss an idea for a training program. Based upon a survey of teachers and following a meeting with his advisory committee, a primary goal established for the year was to improve home and school communications. The group considered various persons to conduct training on parent conferencing techniques, and decided that rather than going outside the district, they would ask me, "their local expert," to conduct it. I was pleased to be considered in this regard, but not certain that I desired to lead such a program. I already enjoyed a good reputation in the district, but knew from previous experience that inservice programs often generate less than positive reactions from teachers. I was concerned that if the training went well, it might not enhance my role in the eyes of teachers, but if it went poorly, there could be negative ramifications for me.

After much deliberation and consultation with colleagues, I decided to conduct the training (and thus to engage in what Gallessich [1985] might refer to as scientific-technological consultation). My rationale was that the program could enhance the quality of consultation sessions as well as further sensitize teachers to their availability. A goal of the presentations I made at the beginning of each year was to help teachers become better consultees. Thus, I reasoned that if I had significantly more time to share relevant skills, I could make a difference in how they approached consultation. In effect, they hopefully would more effectively use consultation. By better understanding problem-solving procedures, by recognizing the importance of accurately identifying problems, and by forming more realistic expectations about consultation, it seemed reasonable to assume that the entire consultation process would be facilitated (see Sandoval, Lambert, & Davis, 1977). Although I was unable to substantiate my hypothesis experimentally, the results in Table 3.1 show that there was an increased use of consultation in Year V. As an aside, we eventually were able to validate this hypothesis and demonstrate that such training can improve consultee problem identification skills (Ponti & Zins, 1990).

In conclusion, marketing clearly is a necessary component to making consultation a routine aspect of an organization's functioning. We may not like to think in such terms, but developing a marketing plan is one of the cornerstones of effective practice.

Overcoming Barriers and Resistances

Without a doubt, the initial resistance encountered associated with the district's conceptualization of consultation was among the most challenging barriers I faced. Even after several years, various faculty and administrators would resurrect the issue of the sensitivity training groups. They did not blame me directly for what happened, but many had their perceptions of mental health professionals altered by the experience. For at least the first two years I continually had to work on building our trust level. Keeping interactions as collaborative as possible and involving consultees in the problem-solving process were the best means to overcome these perceptions.

At the beginning of the case the extremely limited time I had available to consult was a barrier because I could not meet all of the demands for service. Fortunately, most teachers understood my circumstances and a number reacted by letting the administration know that they desired additional consultation services. In later years, demand for service also became a problem when I was unable to meet with consultees within what they considered to be a reasonable time. Some teachers were unaware of the scope of my job and of the number of persons seeking consultative services; thus they sometimes were not pleased when their requests were not acted upon immediately. A contributing factor was the large numbers of students served (it was greater than that recommended by the professional practice standards in school psychology). Thus, although it is sometimes emphasized that a consultative model facilitates the provision of more immediate assistance (especially in comparison to traditional diagnostic approaches), there are limits to how many consultees can be served within a given period of time (see Ponti, Zins, & Graden, 1988, for example of a similar increase in requests for services).

During one year consultation services were somewhat disrupted in one school. A teacher was sued by a student's parents, and a number of teachers were called to testify. Needless to say, the level of stress in the school increased and communication was hampered. Some teachers seemed concerned that anything they said to colleagues could someday come back to haunt them if they were involved in a lawsuit. The organizational climate was altered, and the ramifications for consultation activities were apparent. This incident demonstrates how factors external to the school can have a significant impact on consultation.

Program Evaluation

At noted earlier, evaluation of the psychological services program was an essential component of my initial contractual agreement with the district. Over the five years of the case, various activities were evaluated including consultation usage, process and outcome issues (such as consultant interpersonal and professional skills), psychological reports, counseling, and referral out procedures. Data resulting from some of these efforts are reported in this section. In addition, there is a discussion of how the data were used to expand the amount and types of psychological services provided.

At the end of each year, an assessment of services was conducted using the Psychological Services Assessment Questionnaire (PSAQ) (Zins, 1981, 1984). This instrument was completed anonymously by the entire staff, usually at faculty meetings. Consequently, more than 90% of the questionnaires were returned each year. The PSAQ consisted of items related to three areas: (a) respondent background information, (b) consultation services (e.g., frequency of consultant contact, benefits of working with the consultant, consultant effectiveness), and (c) psychological evaluations. Each year the results of the PSAQ were presented to the Leadership Team and to the Board of Education, and they were made available to teachers and parents.

The data reported in Table 3.1 are from the PSAQ, and indicated that the quantity of consultation services increased during the first three years and then stabilized at a point in which more than 90% of the teachers used them, although they did so more frequently in later years. During this time the emphasis of psychological services changed from being primarily

TABLE 3.2 Examples of Results Obtained From the Psychological Services Assessment Questionnaire

	Percentages of Positive Responses	
Category	*Year IV*	*Year V*
Reported Benefits of Working With the Consultant		
Able to see complexities of problem situation in greater depth and breadth	83	84
Helped to clarify/specify the problem	85	81
Able to see alternatives I had not thought of before	87	86
Confidence in solving similar problems in the future	80	82
Ratings of Consultant Effectiveness		
Able to establish a good working relationship	100	100
Viewed his role as a collaborator rather than an authoritative-expert	95	96
Fit into my school environment	100	98
Respected values that were different from his	92	89

remedial to more preventively oriented. These results appear to be consistent with Caplan's (1970) contention that as consultees become more sensitive and sophisticated in their understanding of psychological issues, their need for and the value of consultation may rise.

Examples of additional PSAQ data are shown in Table 3.2. Of particular note are those reflecting consultee perceptions of working with the consultant. On these examples of PSAQ items, consultees consistently indicated their belief that they had benefited in the areas listed as a result of consultative interactions. Although the relationship of these self-reports to actual behavioral change is unknown, it is reasonable to assume that the teachers were accurate judges of their professional skill development, and that consumer satisfaction has merit in and of itself as a social validation indicator.

During Years III through V, teachers also were asked if they implemented any strategies developed through consultation. An average of nearly 80% responded affirmatively, with 68% rating these attempts as successful, 20% neutral, and 12% unsuccessful. Because a majority of the teachers believed that the consultant helped to clarify the problem situation, it is not surprising that a large percentage subsequently were successful in im- plementing the consultative interventions (see Bergan & Tombari, 1976, regarding the relationship between problem identification and problem solution).

The other consultation-related section of the PSAQ dealt with teachers' evaluations of consultant effectiveness along a number of process or interpersonal dimensions (see examples of items in Table 3.2). This feedback was of interest to the district, but even more importantly, it helped me monitor my performance and to identify areas for my professional development.

The School Board and Leadership Team reacted positively to the accountability data collected each year, and indicated that the decision to increase the amount of psychological services was influenced by these results. I can clearly recall the comments of the President of the Board of Education after the first or second time I presented the data. When I happened to see him the morning after the Board meeting, he said something like, "I know it's extremely hard to evaluate the quality of our work, and few people ever do so for that reason. You are to be commended not only for the excellent results you have obtained, but also for your willingness to try to develop an effective evaluation system."

Another example of program evaluation data pertains to outside referral procedures. I spent considerable effort during consultation each year referring students, parents, and families to outside agencies for services such as personal counseling and visual examinations. Too often they did not follow through on my referrals. Their lack of follow-through represented an ineffective use of my time, and more importantly, a missed opportunity for the child. In addition, my experiences at the CMHC taught me that no-shows resulted in much wasted staff time, which was particularly frustrating since there often was a waiting list for appointments.

To address this problem, I read the research literature and learned that anywhere from 20% to 50% of prospective outpatients fail to keep their initial psychiatric appointments (e.g., Folkins, Hersch, & Dahlen, 1980). Discussions with other school psychology colleagues suggested that they had similar difficulties. A variety of techniques were suggested in the literature to resolve this problem, but it was not clear that any of them had proven superior. Therefore I used suggestions from these and other sources, synthesized them with my own clinical experiences, and developed a systematic method of making referrals. I worked on the assumption that my major task was to get these families to keep their first appointment; thereafter, it primarily was up to the therapist to keep them involved.

To evaluate the referral procedures, I collaborated with one of the CMHC staff and designed an applied research project. Based upon our analysis, the system was found to be highly successful: 96% of my referrals kept their initial appointments, compared to 78% of the CMHC's other referrals (Zins & Hopkins, 1981). As a result of this investigation, I was able to improve an additional aspect of the consultation program. Further, because I became viewed as someone with expertise in program evaluation, I was charged with developing that component of the gifted program that eventually included an examination of the efficacy of the identification procedures (Rosenthal, DeMers, Stilwell, Graybeal, & Zins, 1983). The evaluation data helped us refine several programmatic procedures.

Another aspect of the overall program evaluation relied upon anecdotal reports. During my last three years in the district, I usually supervised a number of school psychology practicum students. They also were placed in several other schools, which in contrast to my district had a far longer history of regular psychological services availability. Nevertheless, it was common to hear the graduate students remark about how surprised they were that the teachers in each building knew me. In their other placements, they observed that most teachers did not know the psychologist. Their comments further substantiated the effectiveness of my marketing efforts.

A final measure of the impact of the overall organizational intervention is related to the point at which I left the district. The administration specifically sought to replace me with someone who similarly could provide comprehensive psychological services from a consultative framework, lending further support to the effectiveness of this approach and to the durability of the intervention.

Personal Reflections on the Consultation Experience and Training Implications

In reflecting on these five years of practice, there are a number of things that I learned about consultation as well as several issues that I continue to contemplate. In this section I share some thoughts that I believe may be of interest to other consultants, to those who train consultants, and to consultation students.

A great deal of the consultation literature reports the results of relatively short-term interventions. However, *a more complete understanding of consultation is acquired after several years of intensive involvement* in an organization, than emerges following more limited interactions. Similarly, a richer experience occurs when the consultant works with the organization on a full-time or similarly intensive basis rather than less frequently. For example, after I had worked with consultees over a period of time, it was not necessary to spend as much time developing rapport, clarifying appropriate concerns to discuss, reviewing the problem-solving process, or dealing with misconceptions. They also learned the importance of collecting baseline data, were able to use a variety of techniques to collect it, and usually brought such information to our sessions. For these reasons the length of sessions seemed to decrease and to proceed more efficiently, which was an outcome that consultees appreciated due to the many demands placed on their time. Without my long-term involvement, however, I may not have been able to observe this outcome. Thus our understanding of the consultation process may be enhanced if additional intensive interventions are analyzed and reported.

Closely related to length of involvement in the system is that this study documents that *durable organizational change takes a number of years to attain,* a fact often noted in the literature (e.g., Fullan, Miles, & Taylor, 1980). Other psychologists frequently asked how I brought about the changes in the Westmont Schools. Although I wished I had some catchy response, in reality there are no simple shortcuts or easy ways to expand psychological services (despite the hope that some seem to have about finding such a solution!). Key ingredients include adequate preparation to undertake the change effort, a clear conceptualization and understanding of systems issues and needs, adoption of an appropriate theoretical framework to guide practice, the active involvement and commitment of organizational members, use of data-based evaluation techniques, along with hard work, patience, and persistence. In particular, it is essential to recognize the complex interactions among the personal, social, and ecological variables occurring in an organizational context, and of the need to conceptualize psychological interventions from an organizational perspective (Maher et al., 1984). Frequently, others observed that, "Well, it was easy for you to make these changes in Westmont because . . . . In my case, it's just not possible. They just won't let me do those kind of things." I've concluded that it is far easier to look for excuses about why such services will not be accepted, to blame others for maintenance of the status quo, or to engage in more traditional activities such as diagnostic testing, than to struggle with consultation issues such as entry, relationship building, long-term program maintenance, and accountability.

Flexibility and a willingness to engage in a variety of consultative roles, depending upon the changing needs of the consultee system, is important to maintaining effective practice over time. Most of my efforts involved joint problem solving, but at other times I became more of an information expert, as when I developed the evaluation plan for the gifted program or provided technical assistance regarding special education due process procedures. As consultants we must continually assess the needs of the system and base our mode of operation appropriately to be most effective. In addition, it is necessary to have content expertise in areas such as applied behavior analysis or program evaluation, in addition to an understanding of the consultative problem-solving process.

Developing a better understanding of the consultation process is a continual process. A noteworthy insight occurred, for instance, after I participated in a consultation research project. As part of it, a teacher and I engaged in weekly consultation sessions, and we kept logs of times outside the sessions when we thought about the identified problem. In reviewing the logs, we were amazed to learn that we both consistently continued to engage in the problem-solving process on our own, well after the sessions had ended. This was a valuable lesson for me as I had often been frustrated when consultation sessions ended before the consultee and I were able to develop a solution. What I learned from the research was that problem solving begins during consultation and continues to proceed after the session concludes. Thus my observation that consultees frequently returned for follow-up sessions with a solution already developed, or at least with a far better understanding of the situation than I had anticipated, could now be accounted for by this process.

The advantage of consultation being non-evaluative was reinforced for me during a discussion I had with a principal. He observed that although teachers found consultation helpful in resolving many problems, he felt that he could engage in the process as effectively as I did. However, he pointed out my major advantage: I was not required to evaluate teachers' performance each year, and consequently, most of them were more willing to discuss difficult, challenging issues with me. His point was well made.

For a long time I attempted to establish "collaborative relationships" with consultees, but over the years my understanding of this concept became less clear. For example, although the term often is used to refer to equality in power status (see Gutkin & Curtis, 1990), I observed that schools put psychologists and most of their consultees in hierarchical positions (e.g., psychologists, guidance counselors, and social workers are paid more than most teachers) (Witt & Martens, 1988), and the parties often differ greatly in their professional expertise. Nevertheless, consultees need to be involved in the problem-solving process and must know that their input is important. Collaboration also appears to be situation specific and should not be conceptualized as a dichotomous construct. As should be clear, the collaboration issue is complex and in need of further clarification. However, consultants' interpretations of it have implications in terms of the type of relationship they develop with consultees, and each of us must resolve this dilemma (see Witt, 1990, and Sheridan, 1992, for interesting discussions). As a trainer, I have found that giving students the opportunity to serve as consultees as well as consultants helps them develop an appreciation of the complexities of this and other issues.

The *importance of data-based evaluation and marketing efforts repeatedly emerged.* I feel quite certain that the change process would have taken much longer had there been no evaluation activities. We are at the point at which we can no longer tell decision makers that we provide a valuable service; we must demonstrate it to them through data-based evaluations and accountability efforts (Zins, 1990). In conjunction with these efforts, there are benefits to drawing upon the expertise of our colleagues in marketing to utilize accountability data maximally and to increase our effectiveness. Specific plans of action with both short- and long-term goals must be developed to enable us to reach as many clients and consultees as possible. Opportunities should be identified, priorities established, goals set, resources allocated, implementation activities monitored, and process and outcome results examined (Connor & Davidson, 1985). Each of these elements should be part of an overall consultation plan.

With respect to training in consultation, *a combination of didactic and experiential opportunities as well as ongoing self-evaluation are critical in bridging the gap between classroom theory and applications in the field.* In this case, the schools initially were paying a high hourly rate to the CMHC for my services, and it was essential that I immediately began my involvement in the district once the contract was finalized. It may have been disastrous to spend significant time adjusting to my new role and not to pursue entry and involvement in the system aggressively. However, it has often been my experience to observe new professionals without much practical experience frequently spend significant amounts of time "acclimating themselves" to their responsibilities, thereby delaying involvement in services delivery.

The peer support group (Zins et al., 1988) described earlier, is a promising approach for continuing professional development. In addition, methods to monitor our professional performance are essential. The behavioral self-management process discussed by Wilson, Curtis, and Zins (1987) is an example of how consultants can engage in systematic self-renewal and self-change, particularly during their training experiences. Graduate school is only a starting point for skill acquisition, and professional growth and development are lifelong responsibilities associated with being a professional.

The experiences that I described enabled me to grow and develop as a consultant and as a trainer of consultants. My hope is that other consultants, trainers, and students will find this review and analysis helpful in their respective roles, and that it will lead in some way to a greater appreciation and understanding of the complexities of this exciting area of professional practice.

References

Bergan, J., & Tombari, M. (1976). Consultant skill and efficiency and the implementation and outcomes of consultation. *Journal of School Psychology, 14,* 3-14.

Caplan, G. (1970). *The theory and practice of mental health consultation.* New York: Basic Books.

Connor, R., & Davidson, J. (1985). *Marketing your consulting and professional services.* New York: John Wiley.

Curtis, M. J., & Watson, K. (1980). Changes in consultee problem clarification skills following consultation. *Journal of School Psychology, 18,* 210-221.

Folkins, C., Hersch, P., & Dahlen, D. (1980). Waiting time and no-show rate in a community mental health center. *Journal of Community Psychology, 8,* 121-123.

Fullan, M., Miles, M. B., & Taylor, G. (1980). Organization development in schools: The state of the art. *Review of Educational Research, 50,* 121-183.

Gallessich, J. (1973). Training the school psychologist in consultation. *Journal of School Psychology, 11,* 57-65.

Gallessich, J. (1985). Toward a meta-theory of consultation. *The Counseling Psychologist, 13,* 336-354.

Graden, J., Zins, J. E., & Curtis, M. J. (1988). (Eds.). *Alternative educational delivery systems: Enhancing instructional options for all students.* Washington, DC: National Association of School Psychologists.

Gutkin, T. B., & Conoley, J. C. (1990). Reconceptualizing school psychology from a service delivery perspective: Implications for practice, training, and research. *Journal of School Psychology, 28,* 203-224.

Gutkin, T. B., & Curtis, M. J. (1990). School-based consultation. In T. B. Gutkin & C. R. Reynolds (Eds.), *The handbook of school psychology* (2nd ed., pp. 577-613). New York: John Wiley.

Kirschenbaum, H., & Glasser, B. (1978). *Developing support groups.* La Jolla, CA: University Associates.

Kratochwill, T. R., & Bergan, J. (1990). *Behavioral consultation in applied settings.* New York: Plenum.

Kuehnel, J. (1975). *Faculty, school, and organizational characteristics and schools' open-ness to mental health resources.* Unpublished doctoral dissertation, University of Texas at Austin.

Lentz, F. E., Jr. (1987, January). *Functional assessment of academic problems.* Workshop conducted for the Hamilton County Office of Education, Cincinnati, OH.

Lippitt, G., & Lippitt, R. (1986). *The consulting process in action* (2nd ed.). La Jolla, CA: University Associates.

Lippitt, G., Langseth, P., & Mossop, J. (1985). *Implementing organizational change.* San Francisco: Jossey-Bass.

Maher, C. A., Illback, R. J., & Zins, J. E. (Eds.). (1984). *Organizational psychology in the schools.* Springfield, IL: Charles C Thomas.

Ponti, C. R., & Zins, J. E. (1990, April). *Changes in consultee problem clarification skills and attributions following direct training in problem solving techniques.* Paper presented at the annual meeting of the National Association of School Psychologists, San Francisco.

Ponti, C. R., Zins, J. E., & Graden, J. (1988). Implementing a consultation-based service delivery system to decrease referrals for special education: A case study of organizational effectiveness. *School Psychology Review, 17,* 89-100.

Reimers, T., Wacker, D., & Koeppl, G. (1987). Acceptability of behavioral interventions: A review of the literature. *School Psychology Review, 16,* 212-227.

Rosenthal, A., DeMers, S. T., Stilwell, W., Graybeal, S., & Zins, J. E. (1983). Comparison of inter-rater reliability on the Torrance Tests of Creative Thinking for gifted and nongifted students. *Psychology in the Schools, 20,* 35-40.

Rothman, J., Teresa, J., Kay, T., & Morningstar, G. (1983). *Marketing human service innovations.* Beverly Hills, CA: Sage.

Sandoval, J., Lambert, N., & Davis, J. (1977). Consultation from the consultee's perspective. *Journal of School Psychology, 15,* 334-342.

Sheridan, S. M. (1992). What do we mean when we say "collaboration"? *Journal of Educational and Psychological Consultation, 3,* 89-92.

Wilson, F. R., Curtis, M. J., & Zins, J. E. (1987, August). *Consultant self-managed behavior change during consultation training.* Paper presented at the annual meeting of the American Psychological Association, New York.

Witt, J. C. (1990). Collaboration in school-based consultation: Myth in need of data. *Journal of Educational and Psychological Consultation, 1,* 367-370.

Witt, J. C., & Martens, B. K. (1988). Problems with problem-solving consultation: A re-analysis of assumptions, methods, and goals. *School Psychology Review, 17,* 211-226.

Zins, J. E. (1981). Using data-based evaluation in developing school consultation services. In M. J. Curtis & J. E. Zins (Eds.), *The theory and practice of school consultation* (pp. 261-268). Springfield, IL: Charles C Thomas.

Zins, J. E. (1984). A scientific problem-solving approach to developing accountability procedures for school psychologists. *Professional Psychology: Research and Practice, 15,* 56-66.

Zins, J. E. (1990). Best practices in developing accountability procedures. In A. Thomas & J. Grimes (Eds.), *Best practices in school psychology* (2nd ed., pp. 323-338). Washington, DC: National Association of School Psychologists.

Zins, J. E., & Curtis, M. J. (1984). Building consultation into the educational services delivery system. In C. A. Maher, R. J. Illback, & J. E. Zins (Eds.), *Organizational psychology in the schools* (pp. 213-242). Springfield, IL: Charles C Thomas.

Zins, J. E., Curtis, M. J., Graden, J., & Ponti, C. R. (1988). *Helping students succeed in the regular classroom: A guide for developing intervention assistance programs.* San Francisco: Jossey-Bass.

Zins, J. E., & Hopkins, R. (1981). Referral out: Increasing the number of kept appointments. *School Psychology Review, 10,* 107-111.

Zins, J. E., & Illback, R. J. (in press). Issues in the implementation of consultation in child service systems. In J. E. Zins, T. R. Kratochwill, & S. N. Elliott (Eds.), *The handbook of consultation services for children.* San Francisco: Jossey-Bass.

Zins, J. E., Maher, C. A., Murphy, J. J., & Wess, B. P. (1988). The peer support group: A means to facilitate professional development. *School Psychology Review, 17,* 138-146.

Zins, J. E., & Ponti, C. R. (1990a). Best practices in school-based consultation. In A. Thomas & J. Grimes (Eds.), *Best practices in school psychology* (2nd ed., pp. 673-693). Washington, DC: National Association of School Psychologists.

Zins, J. E., & Ponti, C. R. (1990b). Strategies to facilitate the implementation, organization, and operation of system-wide consultation programs. *Journal of Educational and Psychological Consultation, 1,* 205-218.

4

Facilitating Change in a Financial Service Company in Transition

DAVID A. FRAVEL

JAMES M. O'NEIL

THIS consultation case study focuses on the dynamics of organizational change in a financial service organization in the early 1980s. Corporate America in the 1980s experienced great turbulence because of market encroachments from foreign competitors, shrinking profit margins, and fierce competition among domestic companies for the consumer's dollar. Financial service companies, once traditional bedrocks of conservative behavior and financial stability, were not spared the trauma and upheaval experienced by other industries. Modifications in tax codes, mergers, leveraged buy-outs, and competition among companies proved onerous to corporate profits. Pressure for return on investment was compounded by heavy capital investments in new technologies to increase worker productivity and lower business expenses.

Many business leaders turned to consultants to implement rapid change. Consultants largely performed analytical and often prescriptive evaluations of business dilemmas involving organizational structure, reporting relationships, cost-benefit analysis, work-flow recommendations, technological opportunities and market segmentation potential. Often, consultation recommendations were enacted without considering their impact where it was most immediately felt—the employee level.

Business consultants can often help organizations remain competitive and survive. Unfortunately, many business consultants have little or no formal training in human relation skills. Many consultants, while expert in labor saving efficiencies and expense reduction strategies, are usually unskilled in assessment of employees' developmental needs. The needs of the employees are a fundamental component of any successful change strategy in business and industry.

Trained consultants from Counseling Psychology and other psychological specialties have great potential to help organizations confront, adapt, and successfully implement change processes. Counseling psychologists can play a vital role in organizations in the 1990s by providing supportive assistance on human-development issues in the workplace that help companies remain both economically viable and humane. In a special issue of *The Counseling Psychologist* entitled "Business and Industry," Osipow and Toomer (1982) specified the multitude of roles and relationships for counseling psychologists in the corporate world. Toomer (1982) found high interest in business and industry work settings for a sample of counseling psychologists surveyed. Even with this interest, Osipow (1982) indicates that "it is remarkable the counseling applications to industry have been ignored for so long" and that the profession has "not expanded and fulfilled our logical role directly in the world of work" (p. 19). Furthermore, Toomer (1982) indicated that "the core of counseling psychologists' effective intervention in business and industry lies in the consultation process" (p. 19).

This case study details a consultation in a financial service company that experienced many transitions and changes in the early 1980s. The first author, a manager in the company and a student in Counseling Psychology, served as an internal consultant. He sought to facilitate change in the organization and implement stabilizing influences on behalf of its managers and employees. This case study describes two years of consultation activity from 1982 to 1984. The consultation was initiated at the request of the Vice President of Operations (consultee), who appointed the first author to serve as an internal consultant.

The chapter is divided into several sections. First, the consultation background is described including the history and organizational structure of the company. Next, the consultation issues are specified and provide a context for why the internal consultant was needed during this particular period of change. Third, the consultation plan is presented followed by a description of the consultation interventions over a two-year period. Several consultation events are detailed in this section using Lippitt and Lippitt's (1986) phases of consultation. Fourth, an analysis of the case using multiple consultation roles is presented. The final section includes personal reflections on the case by the consultant and training implications.

Consultation Background

Organization Structure and History

The company had established a national reputation for selling quality financial investments to individual buyers and businesses alike. A sales force of more than 12,000 members represented the company throughout the country. Sales results depended heavily on both the loyalty of sales representatives and on name recognition of the company's excellence in the marketplace. The company's success further depended on an employee force of 3,500 workers at corporate headquarters who provided customer service to representatives and product buyers.

Corporate headquarters included a chief executive officer, 6 senior officers, 30 division managers, 75 department heads, and 150 line managers. Structural components included: a centralized marketing division of more than 200 employees, a financial accounting division of 180 people, an information systems division of 258 employees, an investment division of 128 investment analysts and a sales support business unit consisting of 6 divisions numbering more than 2,000 workers and managers.

The majority of the workers at corporate headquarters consisted of clerical workers supervised by first-level line managers. The clerical workers supported the company through sorting and delivering mail, maintaining client records, and using computer terminals to record information on client transactions. In many ways, the company management structure, work processes, and tasks paralleled activities in other financial service firms. The exception was that this institution had endured for a century realizing substantial profits resulting from the loyalty and performance of its sales force. This success resulted in decades of stability in its chosen markets and minimal changes in its internal and external organizational structure. Figure 4.1 depicts an abbreviated organization chart of the management hierarchy and structure of the company.

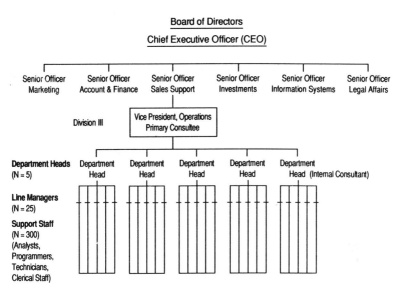

Figure 4.1. Organizational Chart and Management Hierarchy of Company

The chief executive officer (CEO), guided by the Board of Directors, set the policy and direction for the company. The company was divided into six strategic business units, each of which was comprised of several divisions. Figure 4.1 depicts these six business units. The vice president in Division III was the primary consultee in the consultation. Five department heads reported to this vice president. The department heads each managed a separate work group that collectively performed all services required by the division's sales support mission. Line managers and support staff carried out the Division's work load.

Within Division III, 35% of the work force were minorities who represented the single source of income for their families. Educational background of the workers was primarily a secondary school education. On-the-job training focused on the acquisition of keyboard skills and the use of training manuals. The company considered itself a service organization but the clerical work force resembled the production line environment of a factory. Each worker completed a "piece" of the work as a fragmented, functional component of the overall work process. Employees were grouped and managed in teams that performed the same function.

Competition among work groups to increase speed of performance and productivity was encouraged by the first-line managers and reinforced by the department heads.

Most workers in the clerical ranks were skilled in the repetitious tasks they performed but had no idea of how their work contributed to the overall mission of the division. Many were unaware of the division's objectives and goals.

The remainder of division personnel consisted of business analysts, programmers, technicians, and managers. This group represented "skilled" workers who were compensated well beyond the clerical workers. There was minimal social interaction by employees outside their own specific work group. Management training in assessing and facilitating career development needs of workers in all nonmanagement positions was rudimentary, at best. Workers who were technically skilled were promoted to management positions as a strategy to retain them in the company.

Line managers and department heads focused on measuring and monitoring work processes and production output. Superficial attention was given to each employee's career development needs. Employee development meetings were held once or twice a year to talk about individual workers' career development needs. Often, these sessions degenerated into performance appraisal meetings without attention to specific strategies to facilitate skill development. Employees referred to these meetings as "the annual indictment."

The Internal Consultant and Consultee

The internal consultant (the first author) had worked for the company for 15 years. He had served in various management capacities in this division for 9 years and had been a department head for the 5 years prior to the consultation.

The other four department heads managed units of some 80 people. These units were similar to each other in their mission and work groups. The internal consultant managed a smaller group that focused on research of financial issues and evaluation of division financial performance.

The consultant was considered an "outsider" by the other department heads because of his different role. While the department heads managed work process, the consultant managed evaluation of process results. The consultant was personally available to work with the other department heads by providing feedback on division and department results, but the department heads preferred written reports. The consultant had been mentored by the consultee over the years and a strong friendship had developed between them.

The consultee (Vice President of Operations), had risen through the corporate ranks over the years and was recognized as a skilled technician with a talent for technology. He was an affable individual, conscientious in his work ethic, and particularly able to synchronize with others when he felt a sense of harmony in the work group. He enjoyed strong influence with the department heads who reported to him since they admired his technical skills. He was less inclined to deal directly with human resource problems and freely delegated such matters to those who reported to him. Despite the rhetoric of "management team," a term the consultee applied to the department heads, in reality there was minimal collaboration and mutual support among the department heads. Each sought the favor of the consultee and competed with other department heads on the basis of who performed "the best" and thus earned the consultee's favor.

Consultation Issues

In 1984, the chief executive officer announced a new corporate vision that significantly departed from the company's traditional marketing plan and sales strategy. This departure marked a deviation from a path that had remained constant for more than 40 years. The new vision was built on a foundation of aggressive marketing programs focused on meeting the financial needs of affluent professionals. The product line, which had been "plain vanilla" for decades, was expanded at several levels of complexity to respond to market demands. To support diversification of the product portfolio, several subsidiary companies were created to enhance the potential for product distribution and corporate profit. Concurrent with the new strategic direction, the CEO argued that the market focus required a change in the company's name and logo. This new name symbolized the rebirth and renewed vitality of the company with increased prestige in the marketplace. The CEO and the Board of Directors had been influenced to change the company's name and organizational structure because of foreign and domestic competition, rising expenses, and dwindling profits from the product line.

Structural changes in the company resulted in mergers between several divisions and sweeping changes in work groups and reporting relationships. Several previously independent departments were merged together to eliminate duplication of effort, eliminate unnecessary functions, and increase productivity. There was widespread resentment among workers regarding these mergers. Furthermore, employee performance criteria were not specific and opportunities for overtime compensation and merit were not uniform throughout the organization hierarchy. Shortly after the mergers, key performance indicators, including deteriorating work quality and diminished business, demonstrated that the assumed benefits of the mergers had failed to materialize. Division performance was considerably poorer than it had been prior to the merger.

There were several reasons for the performance problems and decreased service. First, the mergers forced many employees to work in new groups separate from their usual support networks; therefore, they were shut off from their personal and social relationships. When this happened, several hundred employees behaved like "conquered people." They arrived at work one autumn morning to find that their familiar work groups had been disbanded and their managers "turned out to pasture" under an early retirement program. Like Jonah in the whale, these work units appeared to have been swallowed whole by a larger, strange organism. The structural changes in the divisions failed to provide a "time out" for employees to adjust to the new groups and develop skills needed for the new jobs. Management lacked sensitivity and awareness that workers would experience negative reactions to organizational change. The mergers were also enacted without providing time for employees to adjust and become committed to the new corporate vision.

There was also increased emphasis from management on expense reduction strategies and leaner operating budgets at the division levels. The new management philosophy was "do more with less" and was grounded in the concept of synergy. This concept maintained that proper organizational alignments would result in greater productivity and more efficient performance. Division heads were held accountable to evaluate opportunities for synergy in their work groups. There was pressure to conserve resources and increase profits. Further, the installation of several new technologies (e.g., computers), intended to improve productivity and service, compounded the division's performance problems. New systems were installed without management providing workers with effective training programs and supportive tutorials on the new technologies. Workers learned them on-the-job or directly from technical manuals. The results were confusion and inefficiency. Daily technical problems produced increased complaints from field sales representatives across the country.

These complaints were addressed to the CEO and the division head was given the responsibility to resolve these problems quickly.

The work environment was tense and uncomfortable. There was also employee turnover forcing those remaining to endure long overtime hours. Employee vacancies were never filled because of a company freeze on hiring to lower expenses. Many divisions were labeled "sweat shops" because of the excessive overtime and demands for increased productivity. Morale was low and there was much worker resistance expressed in high absentee rates, diminished quality, reduced productivity, and worker turnover. The stated consultation issue for the Vice President of Operations, who became the primary consultee, was how to turn this situation around quickly with limited resources.

Five consultation issues emerged from the organizational dynamics described above that shaped the five related consultation interventions. The five interventions were: (a) unclear employee roles that negatively affected productivity, (b) the lack of employee performance criteria, (c) discrepancies in how work compensation and merit pay were administered, (d) limited knowledge of employees' developmental needs, and (e) severe stress and employee dissatisfaction in the organization.

Consultation Plan

A retrospective analysis of the case indicates that the consultation process is best categorized as human-development consultation (Gallessich, 1985). The case study reflects human-development consultation in the following ways: (a) there was an assessment of the organizational needs in the context of organizational change and poor worker morale, (b) consultant-consultee-employee collaboration produced recommendations and planned interventions, and (c) the results of the consultation were circulated and collective solutions were developed over time.

Using human-development consultation, the consultant worked eight months in the implementation phase. The thrust of the five interventions was focused on identifying the causes of one Division's performance problems and the negative effects on employee morale and corporate profits. The five interventions included: (a) clarification of employee roles that affected productivity and quality control, (b) development of employee performance criteria, (c) review of overtime compensation and management merit practices, (d) assessment of employee development needs, and (e) remediation of stress in the organization.

These five interventions were implemented using a variety of consultation roles and approaches. The consultant conducted numerous individual and group meetings with employees, department heads, and the corporate management team. There were brainstorming sessions, joint problem solving, data gathering, needs assessments, written reports, and many meetings with the primary consultee. A final report was written and disseminated in the organization at the end of the consultation. Each of the five interventions is described in the next section using Lippitt and Lippitt's (1986) six phases of consultation.

Implementation

Lippitt and Lippitt's (1986) phases of consultation include: (a) entry and engaging in the initial contract, (b) formulating a contract and establishing a helping relationship, (c) identifying problems through diagnostic analysis, (d) setting goals and planning for action, (e) taking action and cycling feedback, and (f) completing the contract.

Entry and Engaging in the Initial Contract

The CEO received a steady barrage of complaints from sale representatives about poor quality and slow service. The CEO applied increasing pressure to the consultee (Vice President of Operations) to improve the division's performance. Prior to the chief executive officer's mandate to "fix-it," the consultee had attributed the slide in division performance to "growing pains." While he acknowledged that the leading indicators of quality, productivity, and time service showed slippage in performance, he rationalized the problems in these terms: "In time of change, some level of dislocation is inevitable." He expressed confidence that "things would settle before much longer."

In a subsequent meeting with the first author (department head), the consultee expressed his concern that the current organizational shortcomings might be greater than he had appreciated. He expressed his frustration at his inability to "pinpoint the cause" of the problems beyond the "mere fact of change." The consultee asked the department head for his thoughts on the underlying causes of the division's lackluster performance.

The department head had been observing the impact of the merger and was able to respond to the consultee's question. He identified the following issues as contributing to the organization's problems: poor morale due to excessive overtime; the company's policy of not paying overtime to employees above a certain pay level; division employees' feelings that the merger produced winners and losers and many employees perceived they were the losers; insufficient attention by management to specific employee development needs related to skill development; a lack of understanding among all employees as to why the merger was necessary and ambiguity on what the mission of the new division really was; a lack of cohesion among the department heads that did not promote collaboration, mutual support, and sharing of resources. In short, structural changes to accomplish the merger had been installed by management with a "business as usual" mentality. The merger was accomplished without regard for employee needs for support, information, adjustment, and acceptance.

The consultee and the department head discussed the merits of inviting an external consultant to assess the performance issues and make recommendations to the consultee. The external consultant would focus on improving the efficiency of work flow and other operating procedures that were conducive to increased work performance. The consultee concluded that an "outsider" would not be as beneficial as an internal consultant for five reasons: (a) an "insider" would approach the consultation with an established understanding of the division's mission; (b) he or she could grapple with the work process issues that were impacting performance on a deeper level than measurement of work flow; (c) an "insider" would have internal name recognition for access to high-level officers outside the division; (d) an insider could interact with the consultee on a deeper level of understanding and personal loyalty than an external consultant; and (e) an internal consultant would not require appropriations of additional budget dollars since he or she would already be on the payroll. For these reasons an internal consultant was thought to be better suited for more meaningful and full exploration of performance issues.

Formulating a Contract and Establishing a Helping Relationship

A few days after this meeting, the consultee asked the department head (the first author) to serve as an internal consultant. The consultation focus was mutually agreed upon and included: developing an assessment of the factors that were negatively impacting performance; working with the department heads to evaluate and recommend possible solutions; and cycling feedback to the consultee on the proposed or actual change.

The consultee and the consultant arrived at a verbal contract that defined the consultation boundaries. These premises included: (a) an announcement by the consultee to the department heads of the consultant's appointment and responsibilities, (b) a directive by the consultee to the department heads that they were to be available to meet with the consultant at the consultant's request, and (c) a statement by the consultee to the department heads that he was directly sponsoring the consultation at his own initiative because he viewed the division performance problems as "at the critical stage" and expected their support of the process.

The consultant also received authorization from the consultee to initiate and conduct peer consultation with high-ranking officers outside the division. This contact was to develop specific information on remediation opportunities for division problems in the context of the entire corporate structure. These officers included: the vice president of human resources, the director of employee health services, and individual employee relations officers.

The consultee requested that feedback from any meetings held outside the division be shared with him within 48 hours of the meeting. The consultant indicated that he would communicate to those present at all meetings that he was acting on behalf of the division head and would provide feedback to the division head on the content of the meeting.

Identifying the Problem Through Diagnostic Assessment

In the entry phase of this case, the division head asked the consultant to explain why there were organizational problems. The consultant responded with an in-depth analysis citing multiple causes. In this regard, much diagnostic assessment had emerged from the consultant's many years in the organization. Additionally, he had observed how the corporate restructuring had negatively impacted the company's employees. Before serving as an internal consultant, he had completed a problem identification and diagnostic assessment of the situation. The consultant did not need to collect data or interview personnel to pinpoint the problem. It was painfully clear. The division was in trouble and there was pressure from corporate management to turn it around . . . or else!

The consultant was quite aware of the restraining and facilitating forces that might affect the change process. Retrospectively, a force field analysis (Lippitt & Lippitt, 1986) is presented in Table 4.1 to show the facilitating and restraining forces that affected the cyclical, collaborative problem solving of the consultation processes. According to Lippitt and Lippitt (1986) a force analysis "is a model or method for identifying the forces that impede movement toward current goals and the forces that facilitate such movement" (p. 24). Table 4.1 shows 10 facilitating and 10 restraining forces that the consultant recognized before developing the consultation process. The consultant did not diagram this force field analysis during this phase but it would have been quite useful. The consultant did discuss many of the facilitating forces in his early work with his multiple consultees emphasizing the positive and giving the process needed energy.

The challenge was to use the facilitating forces to help eliminate or change the restraining and negative forces causing the organizational dysfunction. Many of these facilitating and restraining forces have been mentioned in the background and consultation issues section of this chapter. Table 4.1 serves as a summary of the organizational dynamics before the consultation began. This force field analysis and the consultant's information base allowed the consultant to set goals and plan for action.

Setting Goals and Planning for Action

The consultant had a "vision" of a robust organizational climate that focused the consultation goals in the context of the consultation contract. Specifically, the consultation plan included information gathering, individual and group meetings, organizational analyses, evaluation, and dissemination of information leading to improved organizational performance.

As the consultation intervention became more penetrating, the consultant recognized a power imbalance between himself and the consultee. The consultant was gaining more power and the consultee felt less power and control. The consultant had a personal friendship with the consultee, but as the consultation developed the consultee's leadership style and interpersonal limitations became apparent producing some personal distance from the consultant. This dynamic prohibited the consultation from being truly egalitarian and fully collaborative in the problem solving (Gallessich, 1985).

As will be demonstrated in the "Taking Action" section of this chapter, numerous consultation interventions and activities occurred. They included: analyses of factors that contributed to the problems, formulation of potential solutions, implementation of new human resource practices,

TABLE 4.1 Force Field Analysis of Facilitating and Restraining Forces Affecting the Cyclical, Collaborative Problem Solving

Facilitating Forces		Restraining Forces
1. The company's distinguished history of success		1. Financial Services Industry experiencing unprecedented stress and change
2. A new, dynamic corporate vision and identity		2. Employee resistance to change in corporate identity
3. A large, loyal distribution sales force	Cyclical	3. New and complex product line implemented without field training program
4. Internal consultant was an expert in division matters and procedures	Collaborative	4. Other department head in division resented consultant's role and authority
5. Division merger had consolidated the strength and resources of three divisions into one division	Problem Solving	5. Division employees were unclear as to why change was needed and were highly stressed
6. Strong corporate training division	in the	6. Budget restraints limited the use of the corporate training division
7. Division head was skilled in technology	Organization	7. Technology was installed without training staff to use the new technologies
8. Majority of employees were long-term employees who felt and valued membership in the company		8. No cohesive, human development training program in career development existed
9. Production demands were increasing steadily, reflecting healthy financial growth		9. Substantial uncompensated overtime was negatively impacting employee morale
10. Management staff was experienced in company business		10. Management did not appreciate impact of change at the human level

and cycling feedback throughout the organization's employee and management ranks. The consultant hypothesized that human-development consultation would increase awareness of the work environment, leading to increased production and improved employee morale. He pursued this model to facilitate an awareness among the work force of the consultee's commitment to solve the problems in the division. The consultation goal was to increase management's sensitivity to corporate practices that affected the quality of life and the division's effective performance.

The consultation process was collaborative in many ways, as illustrated below. Employees were involved directly in organizational assessment through interviews and questionnaires. Several meetings with the consultee, department heads, and outside resources were held with a focus on problem resolution as the broad agenda. Survey results from the employee questionnaires also were circulated to the consultee and department heads to demonstrate feedback of employees issues, attitudes, and developmental needs. This procedure promoted ongoing problem-solving dialogue with the department heads and consultee leading to organizational change.

Taking Action and Recycling Feedback

The consultant used the information in the forced field analysis and his consultation contract to begin the consultation process. Because there were multiple problems, the consultant had to decide where to start. He wanted to select the most important intervention that might positively affect all other issues. The consultant conceptualized the consultation to consist of five major issues including: (a) confusion about employee roles, (b) poorly defined employee performance criteria, (c) unfair overtime compensation and merit raise practice, (d) inattention to employee's developmental needs, and (e) negative organizational and personal stress issues in the company.

The consultant analyzed these problems and judged that the least threatening issue was the issue of employee roles. This particular issue allowed the consultant to test his credibility with the other department heads who were key to resolving the other organizational issues. From the roles issue, the consultant believed that the employee criteria and performance issues could next be addressed. Third, from the clarification of the roles and performance criteria, the consultant could move on to the more difficult overtime and merit practices facing the division. Once these issues were worked through, the consultant hypothesized that needs of the employees could be assessed to enhance their skills and comfort with the many organizational changes that had occurred. Finally, a resolution of these issues and proposed programs could address the overall issue of organizational stress. Each of these issues is described in the next section, which represents the "taking action and recycling feedback phase" of the consultation.

Intervention I: Clarifying Employee Roles. The consultant met with the five department heads to enlist their support and to involve them in the consultation. He encouraged collaboration in the group by highlighting information about the division's poor performance. The consultant intentionally steered clear of performance reports on the departmental level to avoid "turf issues" and what he perceived would be defensive reactions. Rather, he presented overall division results.

He facilitated the group by gaining consensus on poor organizational performance, independent of the performance of any one department. This mattered to all of the department heads because it reflected on the image and the standing of the division as a whole. The reports distributed to the department heads clearly documented unacceptable performance at the division level. The department heads agreed with the consultant's perspective that it was critically important for everyone to work together if the problems were to be resolved.

With the consultant in the roles of facilitator and recorder, he asked the group to identify all the issues they perceived might be contributors to the current situation. This structured exercise was designed to involve the group in the consultation interventions by drawing on the knowledge of each department head. In this way, this process provided an opportunity for the group to collaborate on identifying problems and ultimately recommending solutions. This method of group process followed the corporate directive for synergy, where more can be accomplished in groups than by individuals working independently.

The consultant suggested that the basic ground rule for this exercise would be a "blue-sky" method, where ideas would be recorded without any evaluation of any one idea. The consultant focused the group on enumerating ideas rather than explaining or justifying them to avoid resistance or defensiveness. The consultant recorded all the ideas proposed, occasionally using a probe in order to keep the ideas as concrete as possible. When the department heads had exhausted their comments, the consultant reviewed the list with them. Many of the issues mentioned by the department heads as impacting performance were useful, but most of the problems mentioned were the result of external forces outside the division. Two examples of these external environmental forces included: unrealistic expectations of sales representatives, demonstrated in a "me first" service demand; and a frequent barrage of phone calls from field representatives to corporate headquarters to answer basic questions. These calls represented significant interruptions in the daily work cycles in the division and negatively affected service performance.

The consultant acknowledged that these issues did indeed impact division performance. However, he suggested that because these forces were outside the management of the group, action oriented remediation of these issues was beyond the control of the group. He obtained group consensus on this issue. Next, he recommended that the group begin to prioritize the key contributors to performance problems that were directly related to their management and, thus, more amenable to resolution. He further recommended that the final report of the consultation should include details of those external environmental problems identified by the department heads that did have significant impact on the division. The department heads agreed with this suggestion.

During the meeting, the consultant asked the department heads whether or not the issue of overtime compensation and training could be considered as contributors to performance shortfalls. The group agreed and suggested that these two issues be added to the list. In fact, they recommended that overtime compensation and training become two priority issues in the consultation. The consultant sought group reaction to the idea that vague job descriptions and corporate overtime policies contributed to poor employee performance. The group agreed that unclear job descriptions and the corporate overtime policy were directly related to poor worker performance.

Next, the consultant asked each department head to engage in certain activities over a four-month period. First, each department head would review and revise one of the five key job descriptions in the division for completeness based on the job requirements created by the merger. Second, each department head would share the revised job description with each of the others for feedback. In this way, all job descriptions would be reviewed with the group actively collaborating in the process. Third, when feedback had been received on the revised job descriptions and appropriate modifications made, the consultant would deliver the amended descriptions to the Vice President of Human Resources. The job descriptions would then be finalized according to the company's standard format. Fourth, the department heads were asked to document the current performance standards operating in their department relating to service, quality, and productivity standards. They were asked to share their standards along with recommendations for change with the consultant and all department heads by the end of the four-month period.

This first meeting established a foundation for the consultation including a sense of trust, purposefulness, and collaboration for future group problem solving activities. It also established a critical feedback loop for the department heads and provided valuable information for the final consultation document.

It is noteworthy that when the problem solving focused on global issues, independent of individual department performance, the group was more amenable to working in a spirit of collaboration with each other. For example, when the consultant raised the general issue of time service, quality, and productivity standards for employees that were operational in each department, the department heads acknowledged that new employees may not have been adequately oriented to the division performance expectations. This led to further group discussion that existing standards might need to be revised due to the introduction of new technologies that had added a new level of complexity in the division. The department heads, having reached this level of insight, were agreeable to review performance standards and expectations that had remained unchanged for five years.

Intervention II: Employee Performance Criteria. Prior to the merger, the consultee managed a smaller organization that supported a smaller number of financial products that were processed through one technology system. The merger had resulted in servicing three additional products, supported by three separate and unrelated technological systems. To understand the capacity of the technology systems to absorb work, the consultee relied on work measurement studies analyzing such issues as work flow, volume of sales compared to separate technological systems to perform work. This assessment gave the consultee a high level of insight into the various strengths that the individual technical systems brought to the division.

The consultee possessed considerable knowledge of technological innovations. However, this information was not accompanied by understanding the impact of technical changes on members of the division work force. As a result, there was no modification in the individual performance standards and employee expectations of performance regarding quality, productivity, and service.

The lack of updated standards affected feedback to employees regarding their annual pay increases and had become a sore point among division employees. Without clearly defined performance standards that concretely reflected the complexity of working within new technologies, the performance appraisal became a vague, ambiguous process. Many employees described the process as "unfair and a royal waste of time." Line managers groped for any shred of information that might discriminate employee's performance that might translate into salary increases.

The consultant had previously attended a number of professional conferences during his career and had acquired a number of contacts in other companies of similar size, structure, and product lines. The consultant, with the approval of the consultee, contacted officials in five other financial service companies to solicit information and feedback on work measurement and performance standards for employees in those companies. The consultant was able to obtain sufficient information to design a work measurement model that assessed quality, time service, and productivity.

At a subsequent meeting with the department heads, the consultant shared a work measurement model he had adapted, which assessed quality, time service, and productivity. The model was presented as an opportunity to apply new methodology to the current division work environment. The department heads were asked to consider the utility of the model applied against the "real world" of division work processes and technological systems.

Over the next six months, the department heads met to assess the specific tasks associated with the five employee positions in the division. The tasks associated with each job position were inventoried and a time factor was identified for each task. This meant that the specific tasks in each job description were operationally defined and the average amount of time for each task was determined through careful record keeping. This process followed the work measurement models commonly used in manufacturing companies and provided a baseline of minimum performance expectations for specific tasks for the five division positions.

During the course of the next six months, each department head applied the model to work already in process in their department. Each department head then reported their observations over a three-month period. Consensus among them was reached regarding baseline performance criteria in terms of productivity, quality, and time service for each job within and across the five individual departments in a uniform way. For the first time in the division's history, the same set of expectations were applied to all employee groups, within the same job category, in all five departments.

These performance expectations were given to each employee in written form approximately nine months prior to the formal performance evaluation for merit. In closing out the consultation intervention, the consultant suggested to the department heads that there might be considerable merit in providing employees with quarterly feedback. Progress in meeting performance expectations could be evaluated regularly rather than deferring such feedback until the annual performance review. The department heads acknowledged that this was a useful idea and quarterly meetings were held to provide performance feedback using performance standards that had been given to each employee. As one employee commented after receiving the written documentation of the performance standards, "At last I finally know what the game is. . . . I think, after a while, this kind of information may help me know what the score is."

Intervention III: Overtime Compensation and Merit. A strong area of employee discontent centered on the company's overtime policy. Approximately 60% of the division work force consisted of workers who were eligible for overtime compensation at an hourly rate of pay. The remainder of the division workers, primarily technicians, analysts, and first-line managers were not eligible for overtime due to their positions as salaried employees. Although this group represented 40% of the division population, they represented 70% of the division payroll. Three years prior to the merger, there was little overtime work due to "flat" sales years. The following year there was a sharp upturn in sales accompanied by increasing demands for productivity on the part of the reduced work force. Overtime had become a way of life in the division and, for the salaried employees, this essentially meant working for free.

Because salaried workers were not eligible for overtime compensation, the department heads individually awarded merit dollars as a replacement for overtime pay. Criteria for merit pay were administered independently by each department head. Inconsistent and ill-defined merit criteria were a source of friction and resentment in the division. The consultant believed that the individual creation and administration of this reward system should be addressed as a matter of corporate policy. The consultant scheduled a meeting with the Vice President for Human Resources to develop information on the corporate overtime policy and to determine the potential for any policy change. The Vice President for Human Resources felt that the proper issue to address was the overtime policy, independent of the merit problems.

The Vice President was aware "through the grapevine" of the substantial amount of uncompensated overtime being worked. He expressed concern that the division merit pool was being used for purposes other than its original intent (i.e., to reward exceptional performance, money saving ideas, or creative ideas that resulted in cash flow to the company). The Vice President for Human Resources acknowledged that the corporate overtime policy, as it related to salaried workers, had not been reviewed in several years. He promised to conduct a market survey of the overtime practices of other financial service companies across the country. The Vice President advised the consultant that the survey would be completed and the results available to the consultee within 12-16 weeks of the meeting. The consultant reported the outcome of the meeting to the consultee. He also wrote a memorandum to the department heads indicating that a market survey on overtime practices would be conducted over the next three to four months. The consultant told the consultee that there was considerable discontent among employees regarding the practice of allocating merit dollars to employees as a substitute for overtime compensation.

Each department head had an available pool of merit dollars equivalent to 3% of his or her total salary budget. Each department head recommended a merit award to employees under their management. There were no standardized criteria for awarding merit pay to individuals. The lack of criteria resulted in inconsistent standards and practices for merit awards. Many employees who were denied merit felt their performance was the same or higher than employees who received them. This perceived discrepancy led to considerable discontent in the division.

The consultee advised the department heads that the issue of merit awards should be included in the consultation related to employee compensation. He instructed the department heads to meet with the consultant to develop standardized merit criteria for his review. When the criteria were finalized, each employee would have a list of examples of meritorious performance. The list would also include clear examples of activities that were not considered meritorious.

At a meeting, each department head acknowledged that there was a morale problem in their department regarding the uncertainty of merit criteria. They also agreed that it was desirable to focus on specific criteria for merit awards. The consultant facilitated discussion among the department heads to specify a concrete merit program. After some deliberation, the department heads agreed that using merit as a substitute for overtime compensation was inconsistent with company policy. The group reached agreement that overtime compensation and merit awards should be considered as separate issues. The consultant elicited ideas from the department heads about the criteria for merit. A dollar amount for each activity was assigned to insure consistency between the five departments. Each category listed by the department heads was assigned a "reward" ranging from $200 to $500. Further, the department heads agreed that employees were eligible to receive total merit awards up to 10% of annual salary.

The assignment of merit dollars to a specific performance activity also promoted consistency among the five departments.

In a follow-up meeting, the department heads collaborated in identifying specific criteria for merit eligibility. The criteria included: (a) innovative ideas that led to improvement in time service, (b) innovations that resulted in expense savings that were measurable, (c) innovations that resulted in additional sales or revenue to the company, (d) high-quality work over an extended period of time that exceeded performance standards and expectations, (e) work on a specific project or assignment outside regular hours that was not compensated by the corporate overtime policy.

The department heads collaborated in writing a position paper that was submitted to the consultee. The paper gave a rationale to support the new merit program. The consultee accepted the recommendations outlined in the position paper. The consultant, on behalf of the consultee and department, wrote a memo for the consultee and each department head to sign that was sent to all employees in the division. The memo outlined the new merit program, criteria for eligibility, and the cash value assigned to each activity.

Employees were encouraged in the memo to share in writing their thoughts, feelings, and reactions to the new program. Employees were also encouraged to submit additional criteria to be considered as merit that were not included in the original list. Within a two-week period, six employees communicated 10 new ideas for merit consideration. The consultee and the department heads reviewed the 10 suggestions and 4 of them were added to the list. A new list was distributed to all employees. The revised memorandum also identified and thanked all employees who had provided feedback and additional modifications to the program.

This intervention resulted in employee clarification of the purpose and criteria of the merit program. It also resulted in equitable distribution of merit dollars within and across the five departments.

Intervention IV: Assessing Employees' Developmental Needs. The consultant perceived that employee morale was negatively affected by the aftermath of the large-scale mergers. These changes at the "grass root" level were immediately felt by clerical workers, business analysts, and first-line managers. The new technologies required full technical understanding and the acquisition of new skills. Training on new technical systems had been limited to reviewing a "User's Guide" that had been sent to the company by the external institutions. Despite the best efforts of first-line managers to train their staff in these new systems, the process was slow and painful because each had its own level of complexity. The rapid influx of new technologies created special problems for first-line managers because they lost touch with the technical functions of the individuals they supervised. Those who managed the systems (i.e., first-line managers) lost touch with the reality of the daily work and the actual skills and ability of those they supervised. When introducing new technologies, the company had ignored the needs of managers who supervised employees who ultimately became skilled in these technologies (Goldsmith, 1988).

The consultant discussed these perceptions with the consultee and he arranged for a meeting with all department heads to discuss the issue of employee training. The consultant facilitated the discussion and reached consensus with the department heads that expertise to provide training did not exist in the division. The consultant agreed to meet with the Vice President for Human Resources to determine if training existed anywhere in the company. If it did, the consultant was prepared on behalf of the division to negotiate extra hours of training for the division clerical staff and first-line managers in these systems. The consultee suggested that it would be useful to pinpoint specific training needs of employees and line managers. The consultant suggested that the department heads and consultee work together to develop a needs assessment questionnaire on employee training needs.

At a second meeting, the consultee facilitated a joint problem-solving session with the department heads to develop a needs assessment questionnaire for review by the consultee. A 32-item questionnaire of the technical and clerical workers and line managers was developed. Completion of the questionnaire did not require any employee to sign his or her name. The purpose of the questionnaire was to assess the specific needs of employees and provide a focus for training.

The consultee made minor changes in the questionnaire and asked the consultant to draft a brief letter to all employees in the division. The intent of the cover memorandum was to: (a) express the consultee's interest in supporting the employees in developing skills necessary to do their jobs, (b) encourage each employee to complete the survey and return it to his or her line manager at the earliest opportunity, (c) acknowledge that training sessions would be held for both employees and line managers, (d) acknowledge that new technologies had introduced complexity and stress in the organization, and (e) express management's commitment to supporting employees in the acquisition of skills needed for success on their jobs. The questionnaire was positively received by employees and managers. More than 85% of the work force completed the form within three working days of receiving it.

At a third meeting, the consultant and department heads met to tabulate the training needs identified by employees. Fifteen need areas were identified and were redistributed to all employees to prioritize them in terms of critical training needs. Employees returned the priority areas within one week. The consultant then met with the Vice President for Human Resources to seek additional training support from expert sources outside the division.

The meeting with the Vice President for Human Resources was to review the employee feedback questionnaires. The consultant sent her a detailed summary of the employee feedback questionnaires regarding specific training needs in priority order. The Vice President called the consultant two days prior to the meeting and suggested that the Head of Corporate Training attend the meeting to address the division's training needs. The consultant agreed to this suggestion and further recommended that the Director of Corporate Training be sent a copy of the needs assessment results.

In the meeting, the consultant, on the consultee's behalf, asked what specific training programs might be offered by Corporate Training consultants over the next 6-12 months to meet employee's prioritized needs. The Vice President for Human Resources indicated that she was not able to obtain funding to contract with outside consultants who were expert in the technology systems. She expressed regret that help was not possible because of the budget. The Director of Corporate Training indicated that he could make three individuals available to provide approximately 10-12 hours of training per month for the next 9 months. He suggested that this training be implemented in 1½ hour workshops per week each month for the next 7-9 months.

The consultant mentioned he had contacted training officers in the three financial institutions to seek their help but no human resources could be loaned to the company for training support. However, one of these institutions agreed to send the consultant a more "user-friendly" training manual to the division. The consultant brought the new manual to this meeting and gave a copy to the Director of Corporate Training. The training director suggested that this new manual would be reviewed by his department and, if useful, would become a foundation for the weekly training sessions to begin within the next three weeks. The training director offered to have his staff review the new manual for its usefulness and provide the consultant with the results of the manual analysis within three weeks.

The consultant shared this information with the consultee and department heads through the minutes of each meeting. Memoranda were sent by the consultee to each line manager for distribution to employees indicating the meetings had taken place, the ideas under consideration, and the potential to provide additional training in the near future. The circulation of these memoranda provided a useful feedback cycle throughout the organization. More importantly, a clear message was sent to employees and line managers that the consultee and department heads were responding actively to needs expressed by the work force for additional information and skills needed to perform their work.

Two weeks later, the Director of Corporate Training called the consultant and advised him that the training staff had reviewed the new manual and found it would fit nicely into a training curriculum for division employees and line managers on the new technologies. This information was shared through memorandum from the consultee to the line managers and their work group. A training curriculum was developed by the Director of Corporate Training and his staff. Training sessions were held twice a week for 1½ hours for the line managers and employee work groups. Corporate training staff members distributed weekly feedback forms to insure that training was consistent with the needs of the participants. Ninety-five percent of all respondents acknowledged that the training curriculum and "hands-on" skill development sessions were meeting their needs. Each department head monitored work quality in their department on a monthly basis for the next five months. Each noted a consistent, incremental improvement in the quality of work performed by employees operating with the new technologies.

Intervention V: Remediating Organizational and Personal Stress. In the Human Resource Division, a master's level counselor served as an employee relations officer. Her primary role was to mediate performance difficulties between employees and managers and conduct workshops for employees on stress management, nutritional awareness, and substance abuse. A primary role of this individual was to be a referral source for employees to contact outside professional counselors and support groups.

The consultant recommended to the consultee that it might be useful to meet with the employee relations officer to discuss levels of stress in the division and seek her advice on possible ways to reduce it. The consultee authorized the meeting and did not seek input from the department heads. The consultee told the consultant to "see what you can find out and let us know."

The employee relations officer was briefed on the merger events and subsequent slippage in quality, time service, and overall morale. She recommended that small group meetings be held with employees without their manager present, to provide an opportunity for employees to "vent" and express their feelings and concerns about working in the division. Separate sessions would be held for line managers and department heads and participation would be on a voluntary basis.

Each employee would be guaranteed confidentiality of any information shared with the employee relations officer. After the meetings had been conducted, the employee relations officer would provide a summary report listing common themes and concerns that emerged from these meetings. At each meeting, employees would be told that a summary document would be written after all meetings, but anonymity would be guaranteed for everyone. The report would also include recommendations to remedy the stress situation. The consultant shared this recommendation with the consultee and he strongly supported the idea.

Over the next six weeks, the employee relations officer conducted 18 separate meetings with employees. Each meeting lasted one hour and included 12-14 employees. The employee relations officer advised each group that she was there on behalf of the division head to provide each worker with an opportunity to express concerns about the division. When all meetings had been held, the employee relations officer summarized the key themes from all groups in a report to the consultee that was shared with the department heads and the consultant. Common themes expressed at these meetings were: (a) excessive overtime, (b) a lack of training with new systems and concerns about future job pressures without adequate training and support to develop necessary skills, (c) high levels of stress among all work groups because of limited information about what prompted the merger, (d) concerns about "downsizing" or cuts in the division work force, (e) concerns that additional, unannounced changes would occur at any moment.

The employee relations officer offered to provide a stress management workshop for any interested employee over the next four months. During this period, more than 215 employees, approximately 85% of the division, attended a three-hour stress management workshop. The stress management sessions drew the work groups closer together because of the personal disclosures of common stress on the job. As the result of the stress management training, the new groups of workers became friends and began to have more social interaction on the job and serve as information resources to one another. The employee relations counselor strongly urged the consultee to cycle information and feedback continuously through-out the organization about any future change with a clear rationale for these changes.

In a meeting between the department heads and the consultant to dis-cuss the employee relations officer's report, the consultee informed the department heads that he now expected that bimonthly meetings would be held with their work group to share information and to remain "in touch" with employees' feelings and concerns. He also instituted a prac-tice of each department head having one meeting per week with his or her supervisor.

One of the key themes from the employee relations officer's report was the recurring employee complaint about the demand for constant overtime to achieve production results. The division head had accomplished the merger under a directive from senior management to "do more with less." The consultant believed that the additional work assigned to the new division required a higher level of staffing than the current number of workers in the division.

The consultant arranged a meeting with the consultee and the depart-ment heads to review authorized staffing levels for each department in the division. The consultee shared with the group a report on work measure-ment he had obtained at a recent seminar. The report included a mathe-matical formula for assigning task requirements with staffing levels. The consultant recommended that the group identify: (a) tasks that remained unchanged since the merger; (b) tasks that had changed in respect to added complexity as a result of the merger; and, (c) new systems, tasks, and skills that were required as a result of the merger not required before the merger. The consultee asked the consultant to conduct a follow-up meet-ing with the department heads to discuss these task issues, apply the work measurement formula to the data, and submit a recommendation for ap-propriate division staffing.

At a series of meetings held with the department heads, the consultant presented tables of organization charts for each department that included: (a) authorized staffing levels for all departments prior to the merger, (b) the actual numbers of employees currently working in the division, (c) a summary of all outstanding requisitions to hire employees. Using the task list assigned to the division since the merger, the group constructed a table of organization that reflected authorized staffing. A second table of or-ganization was developed representing what the group considered to be necessary staffing based on the recent merger and a group assessment of new tasks and required skills.

Concurrently, the consultant met with the Vice President of the Sales Division to obtain reports estimating sales forecasts, marketing reports identifying product development plans, and additional sales projections for an 18-24 month period. The consultant shared this information with the department heads for their analysis. This information added credibility to the work measurement analysis that was then translated into a report that was shared with the consultee. The report recommended 14 additional employees over the next 2-6 months to meet short- and long-range needs in the division.

Based on the potential for additional staffing, the consultant, on his own initiative, invited a representative from the Human Resources Division to meet with the department heads and consultee to discuss the employee market in the local areas. The representative advised the group to prioritize hiring needs to facilitate support from human resources. The consultant suggested that a follow-up meeting be held within two weeks with the department heads to prioritize hiring needs and stimulate a positive response from Human Resources.

At subsequent meetings, the department heads reached consensus on the specific job positions that would be filled and in what order of priority within each department. Over the next six months, the division population grew by 11 new employees. As the work force grew and management communication cycles improved, employee absenteeism and resignations from the division dropped markedly. The result was a sharp decrease in required overtime in the six-month period, with overtime reduced to peak volume periods at seasonal times of the business year.

Completing the Contract

After the creation of new job descriptions, the consultant advised the consultee that he (the consultant) felt that the consultation contract had been completed and that no additional benefits would result from a continuation of the consultation. The consultant offered to write a final report on the consultation that would be distributed to all division employees. The consultee requested that the report be presented as a management response from the consultee to individual and collective employee concerns.

The consultant created an eight-page document that detailed 14 general categories of employee concern and discontent. The document identified 112 issues impacting employee morale, productivity, and work quality. The report detailed how these individual issues had been grouped into the separate consultation activities and how each was specifically addressed by management involvement. The report was signed by the consultee and all department heads as a sign of management support and cohesiveness. When the report was distributed to all employees, the consultant returned to his department head position and resumed normal duties.

Evaluation and Outcomes

There was no formal evaluation of the consultation by the consultant. This lack of evaluation deviated from the standard practice of evaluating consultation effects, changes, and outcomes. The consultant made the decision that an evaluation of outcomes was unnecessary since there were many obvious and demonstrated changes apparent from the consultation process. Seven demonstrated outcomes were apparent from the consultation including: (a) performance criteria and quarterly feedback for employees became departmental policy, (b) standardized merit criteria were established, (c) an equitable distribution of merit dollars was established across the five departments, (d) assessment of employee needs occurred and training programs were established around stated needs, (e) department heads documented an incremental improvement in work quality after the training programs, (f) employees met to verbalize their work conflicts and 85% of the Division attended a three-hour stress management workshop, and (g) 11 new employees were hired to remediate the work overload causing employee dissatisfaction. In retrospect, an evaluation of the consultant process and effectiveness would have been useful. The consultant judged that the organization had reached its maximum capacity for consultation interventions and that an evaluation might be counterproductive to the positive processes occurring in the organization.

Case Analysis of Multiple Roles Used In Consultation

The cyclical, collaborative problem solving in this case can be more fully understood by identifying the multiple roles employed by the consultant. The many consultation roles provide deeper insights into what the consultant actually did and the necessary skills needed to promote organizational change and development.

Table 4.2 enumerates the 12 consultation interventions with the roles employed for each using Lippitt and Lippitt's (1986) role continuum. Eight different roles were implemented during the consultation, ranging

TABLE 4.2 Summary of Consultant's Multiple Roles Using Lippitt and Lippitt's (1986) Role Descriptions

Consultation Activities	Consultant Role(s)
1. Verifying Performance Issues to Focus Consultation	Objective Observer
2. Meeting to Assess Company Overtime Policy	Process Counselor and Advocate
3. Meeting to Explore Training and Human Development Programs	Identifier of Alternatives and Linker to Resources
4. Staff Level Analysis to Support Merger	Information Specialist
5. Meeting on Synergy Concept to Promote Mutual Support	Objective Observer
6. Meeting to Initiate Joint Problem Solving Activity	Trainer/Educator and Advocate
7. Assessment of Employee Training Needs	Fact Finder
8. Meeting to Achieve Consensus on Merit Awards	Advocate, Joint Problem Solver, Process Counselor
9. Environmental Assessment of Employee Problems: Stress Management Programs	Identifier of Alternatives and Linker to Resources, Fact Finder
10. Development of Employee Performance Standards	Information Specialist
11. Dissemination of Final Consultation Report	Information Specialist

from very nondirective functions (i.e., objective observer) to very directive functions (i.e., advocate). Each intervention required a defined role or multiple roles to accomplish a specific goal focused on organizational change and renewal. Many of the roles involved sharing, locating, and obtaining information about the organization and recycling this through the consultee or his subordinates. This information exchange role was insufficient to promote lasting change. The roles of advocate, joint problem solver, and identifier of alternatives and linker to resources were required to implement actual structural change in the organization.

Training Implications

A consultant working in business settings needs well-developed skills and coherent perspectives on organizational change. From the consultant's experience, the following recommendations are suggested to future trainers of consultants.

First, trainers of consultants need to provide knowledge about organizational systems and current theories of human development management and organizational change. Multiple theories should be taught because of the many diverse roles and functions required of consultants (Conoley & Conoley, 1982). Second, consultants in business settings need expert group leadership and process skills. Consultants need to be able to develop trust with consultees and positive group dynamics that allow problem solving to occur. Third, consultants working in business settings need expert skills in data gathering, needs assessment, and resource networking. These skills involve more than developing questionnaires and contacting others. Skills required include knowing how to present and use data in ways that facilitate change. Fourth, consultants need to have excellent writing and public speaking skills. Some of the critical developments in this consultation required the consultant to write concise memos to the consultee or other employees. Likewise, there were many situations where the consultant had to address a potentially difficult problem in public and be able to communicate effectively with the parties involved. Lastly, trainers of future consultants need to facilitate trainees' awareness of their own interpersonal processes in the context of the consultation functions. One of the most significant issues for the consultant in this case was working through his own feelings and conflicts to keep the process moving effectively.

Personal Reflections

More than eight years have passed since I (the first author) completed this internal consultation assignment. The intellectual challenge of recreating the consultation history and recalling the myriad details of its activities and interventions has awakened dormant, bittersweet memories and created a strong sense of déjà vu. I am still a member of this organization, and with some sense of irony, acknowledge that for the past two years I have been in the role of division head, which was the position of the primary consultee.

I accepted the consultation assigned in 1982 with only limited knowledge of consultation theories or psychological principles. In writing this chapter, I have felt many an adrenaline rush of "if I knew then what I know now." There have been emotions about how much richer and more effective the consultation might have been if I had been equipped with additional skills. The absence of advanced training and experience in consultation meant the real difference between being helpful (which I was) and being fully expert in the consultation.

I understand now that as an internal consultant I had a particularly heavy burden to bear. As a member of the organization, I was "part of the action." I had a real dependency on continued membership in the organization for my personal and financial security. This brought about the added pressure of living with the implications and consequences of my actions. It meant that the change that occurred during the consultation ultimately had to coexist with my relationship with the consultee and peers.

There is a reality to organizational consultation that involves telling individuals what they may not want to hear and often at a time they least want to hear it. It is inevitable that organizational consultation activities will often lead to conflict and confrontation. Dealing with these conflict issues, as an internal consultant, clearly reduced my sense of personal safety. It also led to temptations to approach issues in a more superficial way.

Further constraining the consultation was my loyalty to the management staff of the company. The consultee was my mentor and I accepted much of what I saw occurring in the division (i.e., employee turnover, absenteeism, deteriorating work quality) at face value without making connections to management styles and leadership that were affecting the organization. I saw the consultation assignment as a "project" to manage and complete in a timely way. This, I believe, caused me to see events unfolding through filters of years of experience as a manager and a member of the organization who was loyal to my management and the hierarchy. This proclivity produced a distinctly less clear focus on the value, needs, and role of the line employee than I have today.

I learned much from this experience about corporate process and the impact of leadership skills. I was able to serve as teacher and educator in the context of my own management experience. I learned to appreciate networking and the need to recognize my own limitations and expertise in solving problems.

A valuable lesson was learned working with change in the corporate setting. The crisis my company faced in the early 1980s has now taught me and other members of senior management that change cannot be imposed "top down" without understanding all levels of the organization and the impact of change on people. The consultation further taught the real value of listening as a process and leadership skill. I also learned the absolute need to be courageous in facing confrontational or controversial issues.

Professional consultants from Counseling Psychology and other disciplines can help focus the challenge of building an appropriate set of employee attitudes and skills. They can also shape more fully developed business processes that recognize the value of human relationships. Consultants can help us respond to environmental and competitive demands by challenging us to focus less on the attainment of some magical template to lay on the organization and more on developing the abilities and awareness of individual managers and employees. For if consultation is a vehicle to bring knowledge and service to modern work organizations (Gallessich, 1985), it is at this level of change that consultants have the greatest opportunity to contribute to the evolution and the transformation of corporate America.

References

Conoley, J., & Conoley, C. (1982). *School consultation.* Elmsford, NY: Pergamon.

Gallessich, J. (1985). Toward a meta-theory of consultation. In D. Brown & D. Kurpius (Eds.), Consulting [Special issue], *The Counseling Psychologist, 13,* 336-354.

Goldsmith, G. (1988). I/S implementation vs. installation: Changing the way business gets done. *Chief Information Officer.*

Lippitt, G., & Lippitt, R. (1986). *The consulting process in action* (2nd ed.). La Jolla, CA: University Associates.

Osipow, S. (1982). Counseling psychology: Applications in the world of work. *The Counseling Psychologist, 10,* 19-25.

Osipow, S., & Toomer, J. E. (Eds.). (1982). Counseling psychology in business and industry [Special Issue]. *The Counseling Psychologist, 10,* 3.

Toomer, J. E. (1982). Counseling psychologists in business and industry. *The Counseling Psychologist, 10,* 9-18.

5 Health Promotion Policy Development in a Hospital Setting

DONALD I. WAGNER

STEVEN P. KRAKOFF

Consultation Background and Setting

HOSPITALS are in a state of constant change. Indeed, it is common knowledge that the hospital industry in the United States has undergone unparalleled growth since the middle to late 1960s (beginning with the implementation of the Medicare and Medicaid programs). Yet, since the early 1970s, the health care system has been plagued with significant deficiencies: (a) lack of coordination and continuity of care, (b) insufficient access to care for selected segments of the population, (c) ineffective government regulation of health care costs, (d) third-party payment systems that have contributed profoundly to the escalation of health care costs, (e) lack of competition among health care providers on the basis of price, efficiency and quality (U.S. House of Representatives, 1981). These problems persist and present difficult challenges to consumers, the medical profession, and public-policy makers. The United States health care industry continues to receive scathing reviews about its inability to deliver cost-effective services, particularly when compared to Japan and other developed countries (Herzlinger, 1989).

Nonetheless, the late 1970s and early 1980s were characterized by a relatively rapid and fundamental restructuring of the American health care delivery system. Hospitals, a principal target of criticism in the 1970s, embarked on numerous schemes in order to respond to the widespread restructuring. Many reorganized in order to develop new health care ventures and provide more comprehensive services. Diversification into outpatient and home care programs attempted to bring services closer to the consumer. Integration into multihospital systems and networks of affiliates was undertaken to obtain cost advantages (such as lower per unit costs of delivering service). Marketing and advertising became very visible as hospitals sought to achieve advantageous positions vis-à-vis their competitors. And finally, the practice of strategic planning—borrowing many techniques from the business sector—became more acceptable and formalized. In turn, the role of consultation was shaped by these events as consultants were retained to assist hospitals in planning for and implementing these changes.

The Emergence of Disease Prevention and Health Promotion

At the turn of the century, most Americans died of an infectious disease (i.e., tuberculosis, pneumonia). Today, our leading causes of death are rooted in the day-to-day life-style choices we make about diet, exercise, stress prone behavior, and relationships. In fact, the leading causes of death over the past two decades have been heart disease, cancer, stroke, and accidents (U.S. Department of Health, Education and Welfare, 1979). These shifts in the primary causes of mortality created some of the new challenges and opportunities for health care providers.

Health promotion was one new service area developed in response to these changing market conditions. Basically, health promotion programs aim to delay the onset of disease, as well as reduce its incidence, duration, and severity. As a discipline, health promotion focuses on reducing disease-linked risk factors that emanate from unhealthy life-styles and the environment.

Hospitals eventually recognized two definite advantages that could be derived from the delivery of health promotion services. First, they could demonstrate unequivocally a hospital's reason for existence: to serve fully the health needs of the people residing in its service area and become a center for "health." Substantial benefits in the form of an improved public image could thus accrue to the hospital providing health promotion se vices and helping to contain health care costs by reducing the need f curative care (Bosch, 1981; Yenney, 1981). Second, there were oppor nities for revenue generation. This was particularly the case where pr grams were offered to private industry (Bills, 1982; Burrow & Smi 1981.)

During the early 1980s, health promotion as a discipline was in its ea developmental stages. A number of hospitals had established progra with several reports of success. Not all health promotion programs we alike, but effectiveness was ultimately a function of several factors: the expenditure of a significant amount of time, effort, and money initial strategic planning and marketing; (b) the development of progra designed for businesses, as an employee benefit or executive perquisi (c) the offering of programs to hospital employees, staff, and their fan lies, before marketing them to other organizations or the public; (d) t emphasis on the program's association with an accredited acute ca hospital; and (e) the availability of an adequate start-up budget for c velopment, staffing, and marketing (Bader, 1982; Burrow & Smith, 198

Thus these conditions served as the backdrop for an urban-based n for-profit hospital that contacted the authors as potential consultants assist in the design of a strategic plan for health promotion services. agreed to participate in an initial meeting to further delineate the consu ing issue. Our intended outcome was to ascertain the potential for ongoing consulting relationship.

The remaining sections of this case study present a detailed descripti and analysis of our consulting intervention. The case study first describ the consulting issues. These issues are critical because they defined t consultation system in which we operated and the corresponding rol that we performed. Accordingly, our consultation relationship was guid by a human-development focus, with a subtheme centered around soci political issues. Our dominant role was therefore as joint problem solve with advocacy and information expertise being of secondary importan (Gallessich, 1985). Following the explication of consulting issues present the process used to develop and implement the consultation pla The process focuses on the dominant human-development orientatic however, it also addresses the subordinate social/political theme throu a discussion of our role as advocates and technical experts for the hospi administration and other consultees. Finally, we present personal refle tions on the entire engagement with concluding remarks about training consultation.

The Consulting Issues

At the time we were initially contacted, the hospital was undertaking a substantial strategic planning effort in order to position itself favorably for what was anticipated to be a turbulent decade. Responsibility for the planning function was assigned to a newly formed Strategic Planning Committee whose charges included the development of recommendations for new construction and facility modernization, along with the planning of new programs and services. A recognized hospital consultant was retained to assist the institution by providing professional planning support to the Committee, the hospital administration, and its Board of Trustees.

Human Development Concerns

One of the principal findings of the Strategic Planning Committee and the hospital strategic planning consultant was the identification of health promotion as an area of new service development. This was not surprising given the amount of attention that was being directed at life-style-related health concerns by the government and voluntary agencies. Health promoting businesses and programs were being developed, and public information campaigns stressed the important relationship between individual life-styles and the incidence of chronic and degenerative diseases. Recognizing and responding to these environmental forces was thus considered essential to the hospital's long-term strategy.

However, the hospital first had to confront two potential obstacles. The initial hurdle was the obvious lack of skills within its managerial ranks that would prevent staff members (at their current level of knowledge and skills) from adequately addressing the health promotion challenge. At the early stages of our involvement it was widely acknowledged that no group of managers or staff had the requisite knowledge of health promotion nor the related planning abilities needed to undertake a determined effort. At the same time the senior-level hospital administration recognized that it would be difficult to hire a group of full-time staff specifically trained in this program area. Anticipated financial pressures resulting from changes in governmental reimbursement practices forced the hospital to proceed very cautiously in this and other staffing decisions. Hence, the hospital recognized the need to retain additional consulting assistance that could develop the abilities of existing staff in health promotion program development, and prevent the need for additional hiring. We readily concluded

that advancing the role effectiveness of key hospital personnel would
a central theme of our assistance.

Similarly, the hospital's senior administrators understood that the ins
tution's long-term needs and financial constraints could best be address
by a consulting intervention that did not create a perpetual need for ou
side assistance. Traditional hospital consultants created a dependent rel
tionship that required an excessive financial commitment by the clie
Initial projects often produced extremely long sequences of engagemen
usually costing the hospital considerably more than would have been t
case if it had simply hired the full-time staff (which our client clear
wanted to avoid). Moreover, our client institution hoped that effecti
development of a managerial and staff group (the principal consultee
would obviate the need for an unnecessarily long financial commitmen
Rather, it viewed our consulting intervention as one focused on progra
planning and staff development, with a *diminishing* need for outside su
port. Thus we also concluded that we would have to work together wi
the consultees in order to ensure that their newly developed abilities cou
sustain the effort as we reduced our active role over time. Our clie
lacked direct experience with and knowledge of this type of project, b
felt obligated to present this directive fairly early in our initial discussic

Social / Political Concerns

Although they were subordinate to the human-development concer
the social and political issues of our consultation presented challeng
that were both demanding and intellectually stimulating. Of particu
importance to our case study is the way in which we became aware
them. While the expectations of our human-development role were re
sonably specific and clear at the outset, the hospital administration w
far less candid about the extent to which we would have to serve as adv
cates for its objectives. We discovered early in the consultation that t
administration expected us to assume the leadership in gaining suppo
from two key constituencies: the medical staff and Board of Trustees.
sharp contrast to the human-development functions that we employ
with hospital managers, we had to position ourselves as technical expe
with physicians and Board members to such an extent that we created
mystique that helped counteract some resistance to our efforts. In add
tion, we had to inject our expertise in selected instances to ensure th
project results adequately offset competitive challenges. These social a
political issues are described below.

Advocacy Concerns. Within any hospital, there is an intricate social and political network whose support determines the success of senior administration. It almost always includes key physicians and board members. The inability of an administration to gain this network's support for its initiatives, and establish credibility, will doom it to failure. Accordingly, an astute administration will identify all points at which it can influence medical staff and board opinion. It will also bring to bear all forces required to mold medical staff and board opinion in a manner that promotes its objectives.

The need to marshal support from both the medical staff and Board of Trustees ultimately forced us to serve as advocates for the programmatic changes being sought by the senior administration. While not made clear to us in our early discussions, the administration anticipated some resistance to our efforts by influential physicians. Because health promotion ultimately aims to reduce and/or delay the onset of diseases, long-term success is likely to curb demand for medical services by physicians. Hence, resistance to our efforts by the medical staff was seen as possible because this group would normally act in its own self-interest. Rather than confront the medical staff directly, and assume the entire burden of its resistance, senior administration would periodically reduce its own risk by using us to formulate and present proposals that were likely to be unpopular. Where Board of Trustees support for the medical staff appeared likely, it would become necessary for us to lobby sympathetic Board members directly (one of whom chaired the Health Promotion Study Group—the group of consultees with whom we worked most directly). This would thus neutralize the medical staff resistance. Additionally, it would begin to develop Board-level support needed to approve study group recommendations.

Less pervasive (and politically less important) social and political networks existed among hospital employees who served on the Health Promotion Study Group. Occasionally we were expected to marshall coalitions among this group as well. Hence, joint problem-solving and advocacy roles would be required in order to effect system-wide change that favored the adoption of health promotion programs.

Scientific-Technical Concerns. Finally, there were continual competitive pressures from another hospital that served our client's target population. This was a comparably sized facility with capabilities essentially equal to those of our client. In addition, a historical animosity existed between both institutions to such an extent that there was a continual preoccupation (undoubtedly among both administrations) with the competitor's probable strategic and tactical initiatives. As a result there was some insistence by our client that the project be carried out as rapidly as possible. We thus had to balance the need for a methodical and deliberate approach that was required to develop a high-quality and well-supported plan, with the need for speed in order to preempt the competitor's entry into the health promotion arena. At times we therefore had to inject our technical expertise in order to facilitate quicker task completion and decision making.

Consultation Plan

Our discussion of the consultation plan is divided into two sections. The first section addresses the collaborative problem-solving process used to work directly with the consultees in developing the health promotion service plan and redirecting service delivery at the hospital. It emphasizes the dominant human-development focus of our engagement. The second section addresses the social and political dimensions of our engagement and our corresponding advocacy and technical roles.

The central portion of our consultation plan was structured around Lewin's three phases of an effective change procedure: (a) unfreezing, (b) moving, and (c) refreezing (Lippitt, Watson, & Westley, 1958). Within these three phases, eight subphases were identified and incorporated into the consultation plan. These eight subphases were: entry, relationship development, assessment, planning and preparation for change, implementation, evaluation, stabilization, and termination. Each of these phases and subphases is discussed in relation to this case study.

Unfreezing

This phase incorporates the three subphases of entry, relationship, and assessment in the creation of an atmosphere that supports change and facilitates an assessment of the existing structure for change. These three subphases are visualized as interactive or sequential depending on the specific consultation situation.

Entry. Entry into this consulting relationship was initiated by an exploration of the hospital's consulting issue. As previously noted the central consulting issue was a desire to formulate a plan for the establishment of health promotion services and develop a managerial and staff group that could sustain the effort following our departure. We were confident that basic agreement existed internally on the consultation issue. We then proceeded to share our assumptions about consultation as well as describe our consulting style to the consultee prior to entering the consulting relationship (Brokes, 1975). Accordingly, we presented our framework of consultation to both the Chief Executive and Chief Operating Officers, and the Director of Planning. Our approach relied on a phased, collaborative problem-solving and planning model (Wagner, 1976). In addition to developing key managerial staff, it sought to put in place a sustainable process and structure for short- and long-term health promotion program planning. The obvious intent was to develop and implement a plan for health promotion services (which was the immediate need), yet allow for a capable core group of managers and staff to continue the process long after we exited. We noted to the senior administrators that the success of such an engagement would require heavy consulting involvement up front, but that this would diminish over time as hospital staff accepted greater control over the project.

We also recommended that the planning process be highly structured (using an accepted methodology that we would adapt to this case) and reliant on a heavy time commitment by all managers and staff whose departments would likely be directly involved with the provision of health promotion programs. Structure was felt necessary because of the innovative nature of the service being pursued and the hospital's inexperience with a human-development approach. In addition, structure would help organize the input of numerous consultees and reduce their role ambiguity as they participated in planning exercises.

The time demands on managers and staff would be significant because of the need for a substantial level of knowledge and skill development. Time spent in planning and development would also help the core group of consultees to become sensitive to the many nuances that are unique to the development of any new venture, thus aiding in the coordination and synchronization of implementation activities. Finally, obtaining ownership of the process and its resulting recommendations was yet another reason for enlisting the involvement of department managers. Our previous consulting experiences revealed that staff ownership, and corresponding enthusiasm and commitment, could be readily obtained when those people whose support was needed for implementation were involved in the planning. Active involvement in planning, along with the heightened understanding of the project details, could also sustain commitment when unanticipated problems arose or bureaucratic obstacles appeared.

The senior administration responded favorably to our framework and recommended approval. Even though the time period of our engagement would be longer than originally expected, the benefits of this more participatory and lengthier process were readily perceived. We also believe that this favorable response reflected the administration's respect for our professional judgment and track record. Given acceptance of our assumptions and consulting style by the consultee, we then agreed to explore the possibilities of a working relationship (Carlson, 1975; Havelock, 1973).

Relationship Development. This subphase was the next focus of our interaction. Our corresponding goal as consultants was to establish the foundation for a healthy working relationship (Havelock, 1973). We suggested that the hospital establish a Health Promotion Study Group. The group would comprise the core consultees with whom we could work directly in accomplishing our assignment. Our suggestions regarding group membership were then requested and followed (again a reflection of deference to our technical expertise). The group would be chaired by a member of the hospital's Board of Trustees. It also included the hospital managers and staff whose long-term role effectiveness would be crucial to the ongoing development and operation of health promotion services. Representatives from the departments of nursing, dietetics, physical therapy, speech and hearing, staff development, public relations, and administration were selected to serve. Finally, in order to broaden support within the community, the group also included two local dentists, two staff physicians, a community-based sports medicine therapist, and a YMCA program staff member.

An initial meeting of the Study Group was subsequently convened. During this meeting we achieved several critical objectives in relationship development. We accomplished this through the following procedures. First, we clarified our conceptual framework to the consultees (Brokes, 1975). We then sought consensus among the consultees to work only on issues that were identified within the system, not on issues that were of a personal nature (D. Kurpius, personal communication, September, 30, 1975). We believed that this would be particularly important because of the fragmented nature of the typical hospital organization and the frequent inclination toward turf building. This was likely to be exacerbated by the fact that our client organization contained two separate hospital facilities. Thus we were concerned not only with team building and cohesion within each separate facility, but also with the suppression of rivalries and en-hanced coordination between the two operations. Next, we attempted to form the basis for a trusting, open, and honest relationship by modeling these qualities with the consultee (Caplan, 1970). This was done in the first meeting as well as in all other meetings and interactions with the con-sultees. Finally, we identified the specific roles of the consultees and our-selves (Havelock, 1973). A variety of techniques that are described by Havelock (1973) were utilized to accomplish these objectives. Included in these techniques were: authentic feedback, collaborative action in-quiry, confrontation, group observation, and linkage development. At the conclusion of this subphase we developed a formal written agreement that identified the consultants' scope of work and responsibilities, the respon-sibilities and roles of the consultee, the time line for performance of the consultants' responsibilities, the amount and method for disbursement of consultant compensation, and various other points of consideration.

Assessment. Assessment of the needed or desired changes was incor-porated into a health education planning approach (Green, Kreuter, Deeds, & Partridge, 1980). This approach also incorporated the basic components of a marketing analysis. The purpose of the market analysis was to iden-tify key health problems and health promotion service opportunities in which the hospital had the ability to develop a competitive advantage.

A series of meetings with the consultees focused specifically on this market analysis. Since these were the first consultation activities in the actual planning process, and the ones on which the first critical judgment of our credibility would be based, success here was essential. Moreover, we had to engender a significant level of participation from the study group members yet move expeditiously to the next phases of the project.

We presented a fairly structured but general schema for conducting the analysis to the entire study group. The level of structure allowed group members to grasp quickly the broad dimensions of the effort we were beginning to undertake. It also helped them organize their thoughts so that critical discussion could identify gaps, impracticalities, and other revi-sions that might be needed in the analytical phase. At this early stage of the engagement, the study group looked to us to provide an "expert-prescriptive" approach to the analysis. We fully expected this and had pre-pared the schema with this knowledge in mind. Nonetheless, we believed that it would be essential to move very rapidly into a collaborative, cy-clical mode. As a result, the study group was quickly divided into three distinct subgroups, each of which was to undertake a separate component (or diagnosis) of the analysis. The three components were: (a) a social and epidemiological diagnosis, (b) a behavioral diagnosis, and (c) an educational diagnosis (Green et al., 1980). As consultants, we were to serve as advisors to each group. However, roles were clearly defined so that our function was to provide advice, answer questions, and give only general guidance to group members in the conduct of these analyses. The labor intensive work involving data collection, analysis, and interpretation was the responsibility of study group members.

Within each subgroup, we used our skills and expertise to assist our consultees in the execution of the diagnoses. In a series of meetings with each subgroup, we conducted a second review of the information we needed to do the analysis. The work for each subgroup was then structured into a more detailed work plan as shown in Table 5.1.

In order for each subgroup to complete its diagnosis, the analytical tasks were specified in a manner that focused members' efforts on achieving clear, quantifiable objectives. This was done to ensure that the necessary work was completed, and to give the subgroup members some sense of gratification as they worked through this exercise. Accordingly, each subgroup's objectives were tailored to the unique purpose of the particular diagnosis. For example, the social and epidemiological diagnosis addressed quality of life concerns and the major health problems affecting our client's service area population. The corresponding analysis objectives therefore focused on completing assessments of such things as demographic trends, housing conditions, vital statistics of disease incidence and prevalence, and unemployment levels. The behavioral diagnosis addressed the identification of health practices that appeared to be related to the health problems identified in the social and epidemiological diagnosis. And the corresponding analysis objectives focused on creating an inventory of behaviors that helped explain how health services were being used, how health behaviors contributed to significant health problems, and the life-style risk factors that needed to be addressed in future programs. Finally, the educational diagnosis focused on available health promotion resources in the service area. Corresponding analysis objectives thus addressed the need to identify service gaps and opportunities, how the area's health personnel hindered or helped in resolving health behavior problems, potential competitive pressures, and important factors within in the area population, (e.g., health knowledge, attitudes, and values) that caused health behavior problems.

TABLE 5.1 Subgroup Work Plan for Market Analysis Diagnoses

Tasks	Measures and Comparisons	Information Sources
Explication of all analysis objectives to guide each subgroup effort	Collection and analysis of all quantitative data categorized as follows:	Identification of all primary and secondary data sources to be consulted
	Social and Epidemiological Diagnosis • Quality of life • Demographics • Vital statistics • Public health indicators • Population growth	
	Behavioral Diagnosis • Demand for medical services • Diagnosis of health behavior problems • Documented health conditions and related life-style risk factors	
	Educational Diagnosis • Availability and accessibility of resources • Attitude and behavior of health and other key personnel • Knowledge, attitudes, and values of target population segments	

SOURCE: Adapted from Green, Kreuter, Deeds, and Partridge, 1980.

The last portion of each subgroup's work plan related to the identification of information sources needed to complete each diagnosis. Each subgroup identified critical sources of information that had to be consulted to carry out analyses, conduct any inventories, and formulate conclusions. For example, the group conducting the social and epidemiological diagnosis utilized information from health department, planning commission, and other relevant public agency, documents. The other groups relied in a similar fashion on available publications and reports, or gathered their own original information.

We were particularly judicious in providing technical advice to the subgroups. Through questioning and probing of subgroup members, we ensured that the three diagnoses were sufficiently thorough and that no critical tasks were left unidentified. We were somewhat surprised that technical advice on measures and comparisons, and data sources, was not required to an excessive degree. There seemed to be at least one member within each subgroup who had some knowledge and familiarity in these areas. Thus, over a period of several weeks, the subgroups completed their tasks. And by providing technical expertise and structure, in combination with well-defined analytical exercises, we were able to convert expectations for a more prescriptive role on our part into three highly participatory and active analysis exercises carried out by the consultees.

The interest level of the consultees was extremely high as evidenced by one particular anecdote. Two members of one subgroup were registered dietitians (each representing one of the two hospital facilities). Their interest was so high that their initial time commitment nearly became excessive. Eventually, their supervisor intervened with senior administrators on the study group in order to reduce their level of involvement. A mutually satisfactory arrangement was negotiated that still allowed the dietitians to participate but at a level that did not divert attention from their other duties.

The *social and epidemiological diagnosis* focused on broad measures of health. General indicators of social problems, demographic data, vital statistics and public health problems formed much of the basis for this diagnosis. The primary findings of this diagnosis were:

1. The rapid population growth that was experienced during the 1970s was expected to taper off and reach a growth rate of 3% by 1984.

2. Specific municipalities and townships where population shifts were especially pronounced were identified.

3. Five social problems that impact on the service area quality of life were identified. They included: (a) unemployment, (b) a high percentage of the population that was living below the poverty level, (c) turnover and absenteeism among area employees, (d) low levels of hourly wage employee productivity, and (e) stressful living conditions.

4. Death rates for the area's population were compared to state and national rates. This comparison revealed several concerns: death rates from arteriosclerosis and suicide exceeded state and national rates; death rates for cancer and accidents exceeded national rates; while mortality rates for cardiovascular disease, diabetes, respiratory disease, and cirrhosis of the liver generally approached U.S. rates. As such, the life-style risk factors associated with each of these causes of death were explicated for program planning purposes.

The *behavioral diagnosis* focused on the ways in which the target population utilized the health system. Indicators of the demand for medical services, final diagnoses, patient origin, and the extent to which health services were used properly, constituted the basis for this analysis. The results of this analysis enabled the identification of inferences about major health behaviors and life-style risk factors of the populations. Also, this analysis provided data for the initial identification of potential health promotion services. The primary results of this diagnosis are summarized as follows:

1. Of the two inpatient facilities that were operated by the hospital, one reflected a significantly lower mean patient age. This indicates a probable difference in the mix of potential health promotion services that could be offered at each facility.

2. A high percentage of inpatient admissions at one of the two sites had their origins in emergency room visits. This high usage of the emergency room facilities proved extremely costly and constituted an inappropriate use of important service. Lack of primary care physician services, or lack of public knowledge regarding the appropriate use of the emergency room, were two plausible explanations for this phenomenon. Additional physician services and/or public educational programs on appropriate utilization of health facilities were indicated as potential needs.

3. An examination of the most prevalent inpatient and outpatient diagnoses supported the findings of the social and epidemiological diagnosis. The risk factors associated with each of these diagnoses were then explicated for program planning purposes as shown on Table 5.2. The left column identifies the most significant causes of death (verified through vital statistics and hospital diagnoses) of the hospital's service area population. The right column identifies the behavioral and nonbehavioral risk factors that contribute to these causes of death. The identification of risk factors was particularly significant because reducing these risk factors would ultimately provide the focus for future health promotion programs. The client and study group were particularly concerned about those risk factors that were behavioral in nature, and that could be reduced through life-style changes among the area population (as well as medical treatment in some cases.) Those behavioral risk factors that were most changeable through health promotion programs would then receive relatively high priority. For example, the risk factors associated with heart disease are very amenable to behavior change interventions. By contrast, only two of the identified risk factors associated with accidents are

TABLE 5.2 Health Conditions and Risk Factors

Cause of Death	*Risk Factors*
Heart disease	Smoking
	Elevated blood cholesterol
	Lack of exercise
	Hypertension
	Diet
	Diabetes
Cancer	Smoking
	Environmental carcinogens
	Diet
	Worksite carcinogens
	Alcohol
Other accidents (not motor vehicle)	Alcohol and drug abuse
	Smoking (resulting in fires)
	Product design
	Handgun accessibility
Stroke	Hypertension
	Stress
	Smoking
	Elevated blood cholesterol
Suicide	Stress
	Alcohol abuse
	Drug abuse
Cirrhosis	Alcohol abuse
	Influenza and pneumonia
	Smoking
Diabetes	Obesity

behavioral in nature (alcohol and drug abuse, and smoking); thus, health promotion interventions aimed at reducing serious accidents would only constitute partial solutions to this problem.

The *educational diagnosis* focused on the existing system of organizations and individuals that provide health promotion services. Specifically, this diagnosis identified health promotion programs that were currently operating in the target area and explicated competitive pressures as well as potential collaborative relationships. Four key findings were reported by this subgroup:

1. A variety of existing health promotion programs were identified within the target area. These programs were provided in the following settings: schools, public agencies, health care providers, and community and voluntary agencies.

2. The major competitive threats in the provision of health promotion services were posed by other area hospitals. Other hospitals within a broader service area had initiated health promotion programs and were expected to make rapid progress in further developments.

3. The primary areas in which potential collaboration might occur were in the areas of: cardiovascular fitness, low back pain prevention and rehabilitation, stress management, and emotional wellness. Agencies such as the YMCA and the community mental health center were considered likely to welcome joint sponsorship of future programs.

4. Local organizations were identified that could provide reinforcement of hospital ventures in health promotion. Local media groups (i.e., newspapers, radio and television stations) were considered potential sources of free news coverage and public service announcements. Also, voluntary health organizations such as the American Heart Association and the American Cancer Society were considered in terms of their potential assistance in the form of educational and information resources.

These three levels of diagnosis enabled the identification of major health risk factors that served as the focus of programmatic recommendations.

During these assessment stages, the consultants served in roles of technical advisors, trainers, and process observers. In the role of technical advisors we helped design the assessment process. Likewise, as trainers we provided an orientation to the major aspects of health education program development and social marketing techniques. Then, as process observers we oversaw the work of the three subgroups that conducted each respective level of diagnosis.

As consultants, we engaged the consultees in a process that enabled the assessment of key factors that are important in the development of health promotion programs (Havelock, 1973). Also, our efforts were directed at defining programs behaviorally in order to facilitate the identification of potential interventions. In addition, we assessed the following factors as part of our process observer role: (a) group ownership of potential program areas; (b) probable sources of support and resistance to potential changes (Havelock, 1973); and (c) prevailing norms, decision-making processes, and the locus of policy formulation activities in the hospital (Blocher, 1975).

Moving

In accord with Lewin's theory of Force Field Analysis, this phase was directed at developing new response patterns in the hospital (Lippitt et al., 1958). In this case, the new response pattern would be in the form of a plan for the implementation of health promotion services. The goal of this phase was to utilize the assessment data to formulate a plan that included short- and long-range goals, identification of target markets, and definition of major programmatic events (i.e., designation of program leadership) that needed to occur prior to the initiation of a health promotion program. Two subphases were involved in the development of this phase. They were: (a) planning and preparation for change and (b) implementation.

Planning and Preparation for Change. This subphase was considered to be one of the most critical aspects of this total consulting process. As consultants, our responsibility was twofold. First, we had to develop a process that would enable the Health Promotion Study Group to analyze the subgroup data and design an implementation plan. Second, given our content knowledge, we were better informed about alternative health promotion program options and therefore we were requested to generate program options. Consequently, we selected the following process to guide the Study Group during this phase. First, we helped the consultees identify specific measurable objectives for the health promotion program (Blocher, 1975; Havelock, 1973). Each objective was based on data acquired during the assessment phase. Also, each objective was identified as being either a long-term or short-term objective. Alternatives were then identified for the achievement of each objective. Based on the identified structure for change, with its inherent strengths and limitations, the Study Group identified the costs and benefits of each alternative and ranked them in order of priority. A tentative time line and the projected costs for each priority were delineated and a model for eventual program evaluation was constructed.

Table 5.3 presents a summary of the format used to describe both long- and short-term objectives. Each program objective statement identified a specific type of intervention that was needed to address the life-style risk factors associated with a particular disease or mortality condition. These risk factors were identified in the behavioral diagnosis and are shown on Table 5.2. Each objective also stated the specific disease or cause of mortality whose incidence was deemed to be inappropriately high among the population in our client's service area. For program development and

TABLE 5.3 Proposed Format for Long-Term and Short-Term Promotional Program Objectives

---

Program Objective

Specific type of program needed to address the risk factors associated with a particular disease or mortality condition noted directly below (e.g., a nutritional program to address heart disease risk factors).

Disease or Mortality Condition

Specification of a particular health condition that was identified in the analytical phase and noted in Table 5.2:

- Heart disease
- Cancer
- Accidents
- Stroke
- Suicide
- Cirrhosis
- Diabetes

Age Segment

Selection of some combination of the following:

- Preschool child (1-5)
- School child (6-11)
- Adolescence (12-17)
- Young adulthood (18-24)
- Young middle age (25-39)
- Older middle age (40-59)
- Elderly (60-74)
- Old age (75 +)

Type of Client

Identification of a client that might purchase or use the program, including:

- Nonprofit organizations
- Businesses
- Schools
- Government agencies

Geographic Segment

Identification of which of the client's hospitals would serve as the base for the program.

---

marketing purposes, the age segments most likely to be experiencing the high levels of disease risk were identified from a list of eight possibilities; in addition, a likely client or customer group was also identified. Finally, each objective statement identified a specific geographic area whose population would be served by the health promotion program, and which of the client's hospitals would serve as the base for the activity.

We utilized a variety of techniques to facilitate the collaborative nature of this process. Included as techniques were: task analysis, brainstorming, group decision making, and values clarification (Simon, Howe, & Kirschenbaum, 1972). In order to assist the Study Group members, and balance the level of input between ourselves and this group of consultees, we provided structured training in health promotion program design that was supplemented with case study literature from other programs in the country. Many of the Study Group members conducted their own search for relevant case study material and took the initiative to consult with health promotion program managers in other areas of the country. At times, small subgroups or committees were formed to explore a specific area of program need. This procedure was relatively unstructured with group members deciding for themselves to split off and return with recommended program objectives. Sometimes our input was requested in these sessions; at other times these groups were formed (often when we were not even on site) and the work completed without our input until it was delivered to the entire Study Group.

The major outcomes of this planning effort are summarized as follows. Long-range objectives were developed in order to address disease and/or mortality conditions; these objectives also targeted specific population segments. Target population segments were subcategorized by age, type of client, and geographic location.

In general, long-range objectives focused on reducing the prevailing life-style risk factors that were identified during the assessment. Those that did not focus on risk reduction were related to developing community awareness of health promotion needs and programs, an orientation to basic health promotion concepts, strategies for working cooperatively with other organizations, and general health education activities.

Five major client groups were defined as potential users of health promotion services. They included: (a) nonprofit organizations, (b) government agencies, (c) private businesses, (d) schools, and (e) the general public. Health promotion programs designed for area employers and employees involved the first three client groups. These programs were directed at age segments of 18 and above, (i.e., the primary working population). School-based programs, on the other hand, were directed at students below 18 years of age. Finally, programs recommended for the general population were not focused on a specific age segment. Potential beneficiaries of the general population program were considered to represent a wide cross-section of the population.

Health promotion programs that were based at the worksite constituted a significant portion of the recommendations from the Study Group. This recommendation was in keeping not only with data from the assessment but also in accord with the national trends noted earlier in the chapter introduction. In addition, the consultants emphasized to the consultees the importance of the hospital providing the same worksite programs for its own employees. This point could not be overemphasized as a critical determinant of overall effectiveness. In essence, by initiating programs with their own employee base they could pilot test new programs in a relatively safe environment, while enhancing their image in the community and with prospective business clients. They could also facilitate the introduction of a new service venture to their employees in a manner that encouraged ownership through participation.

In general, it was recommended that worksite-based programs include the following components:

1. An educational orientation to health promotion for both management and employees.
2. An analysis of health risks through a computerized health hazard appraisal or other cost-effective method.
3. The design and conduct of health promotion programs in accord with identified health risks.
4. Evaluation of the program to determine its effectiveness, followed by any required revisions.
5. Environmental supports that encouraged life-style changes. This component involved employee support groups, cafeteria programs that supported nutritious food selection, provision of recreational facilities, and a library with health-related materials.

School-based programs were believed to be extremely valuable because of their potential ability to increase health knowledge as well as influence health promotive behaviors. Typically, school programs did not generate revenue. Hence, we recommended that the hospital consider obtaining external grant support for these programs. It was recommended that the hospital assist local schools in health education programming through the following measures:

1. Consultation on health curriculum development.
2. Development of in-service training programs for teachers, counselors, school psychologists, nurses, and other related personnel.

3. Development of programs to identify children with health problems such as hearing loss or substance abuse.

4. Development of referral mechanisms so that high risk students could be directed to the hospital for related health services.

Finally, recommendations for health promotion programs that serve the population at large were delineated. These long-range objectives centered on participation in community-based health fairs, use of area-wide media as a way of disseminating health messages and promoting hospital sponsored health promotion programs, and sponsoring participatory programs that could increase the community's awareness of health promotion. This last category included events such as competitive and "fun" fitness projects (i.e., swimming, running), school projects to develop safety slogans, and other related programs.

In terms of short-term objectives, the basic goals were: (a) to develop an awareness of the hospital's efforts in health promotion among its employees and staff as well as the general public; (b) to stimulate interest in the hospital's health promotion activities among its employees and staff, and the general public; (c) to encourage people to participate in health promotion programs on a low risk, trial basis; and (d) to gain the community's acceptance of the hospital's role as the primary provider of health promotion services in the area. To this end, 42 short-term, low-cost objectives were recommended. The overwhelming majority of these recommendations focused on activities for hospital management, employees, and their families. As noted earlier, the provision of these programs "in house" before offering them on a larger scale within the community was highly recommended.

A small number of community-based programs were included in the recommendations for short-range objectives. They dealt with the development of a plan for the use of area-wide media, pilot tests of small-scale worksite programs, conducting preventive dental health programs with school age children, and community events that centered around health issues. Consensus, on both the short- and long-term objectives, was reached by the Study Group and the process proceeded to the next subphase.

Implementation. The design of an implementation strategy was the next step. This constituted the design of an action plan for initiating the Study Group's recommendations (Havelock, 1973). We recommended that, as the Study Group developed this plan, they bear in mind the need to obtain Board of Trustee involvement, develop an approach for pilot testing of new services, create a plan for the evaluation of process, impact, and outcome dimensions, and the need for a technical support system during implementation. Nine tasks were identified, along with a suggested time line and resource projections, as part of the implementation strategy:

1. Gain policy commitment from the Board of Trustees to implement the acceptable Study Group recommendations.
2. Conduct a nationwide search for a health promotion program director (who would represent the only newly hired manager).
3. Hire the health promotion director.
4. Appoint a health promotion advisory committee to assist in the ongoing development of the program.
5. Appoint an interim health promotion program coordinator to oversee implementation of the short-term objectives, while the search for a director took place.
6. Implement the short-term objectives.
7. Develop an integrated delivery system for the phased marketing and implementation of selected health promotion programs (including service, pricing, promotion, and distribution strategies).
8. Develop and implement an evaluation plan for the recommended health promotion programs (Opatz, 1987). The first step in this procedure dealt with the design of the evaluation, including an assessment of the program's soundness, the identification of key performance measures and comparisons, methods for collecting evaluation data, and the development of a process for using the evaluation information. We recommended that the evaluation plan should be consistent with research that suggested evaluating health promotion programs along process, impact, and outcome dimensions (Green et al., 1980). We believed this would facilitate the ease of interpreting the evaluation findings and improve the acceptance of those findings to entities external to the hospital (such as scientific groups and government funding entities).
9. Development of a plan for dissemination of program findings through public presentations, journal publications, and research monographs.

Throughout these phases we enjoyed a collaborative relationship with the consultee. Indeed, we were able to provide technical input while guiding a participatory decision-making process that promoted ownership of the outcomes. However, at this point in our relationship with the consultee, an unanticipated event occurred that presented a significant challenge. The Chief Executive Officer (CEO) of the hospital announced that she was leaving in order to assume a new position in another setting. Consequently, a new CEO was appointed and the task of building a new relationship began. Likewise, the new CEO had to be integrated into what had become a very cohesive and cooperative planning group. Needless to say, issues around program ownership prevailed.

We decided to engage the new Chief Executive Officer in the same dialogue that we explored during the entry and relationship phases of this consultation. This enabled us to form a working relationship and secure continuing support for our consultation plan. We then entered into the final phase of our consultation.

Refreezing

Lewin (Lippitt et al., 1958) stressed the importance of the refreezing phase of change as the solidifying experience for the affected organization. The primary purpose of this phase is to stabilize and integrate the changes into the client system. For our purposes, we divided this phase into three subphases. Those subphases were evaluation, stabilization, and termination.

Evaluation. The evaluation of our consulting effort was clearly revealed in the events that immediately followed the completion of the Study Group's task. The short- and long-range objectives were presented to the Board of Trustees at a meeting that included the new Chief Executive Officer. We made a brief presentation that highlighted the written report that had been distributed in advance of the meeting. We emphasized the programmatic recommendations along with the projected timetable and resource requirements. The report was accepted unanimously by the Board of Trustees and an existing staff member was named to serve in the interim coordinator's role. This staff member had no formal training in health promotion and little experience in health promotion programs. Also, the coordinator was not relieved of any existing duties. After the meeting we were approached by the Chief Executive Officer and asked to extend our working agreement with the hospital for an additional year. This request was made in light of the interim coordinator's inexperience and desire to postpone the search for a full-time health promotion director. The desire to postpone the search was connected to the overriding hospital concern not to increase the full-time equivalent base during a somewhat austere financial period.

After considerable discussion we formed a new agreement that placed us in a technical assistance and expert consultant role. Our primary tasks were to design and oversee the implementation of an employee program on health promotion, work with the dietary department to implement short-term objectives in the cafeteria and vending areas, and provide general technical assistance in other program areas.

At the direction of the new CEO, the Study Group on Health Promotion was dissolved following Board of Trustee acceptance of their report. Likewise, a search for a full-time director was not initiated during the first year of implementation. Despite efforts by the coordinator to move the program forward, the overwhelming demands of prior responsibilities along with the new duties of the coordinator's role proved too taxing.

Stabilization. During the stabilization period, it was hoped that the desired changes would be integrated into the client system (Havelock, 1973). This subphase should have provided an opportunity for the client system to practice the new changes, develop a feedback system for on-going program development, and confront residual resistance to change.

However, without the support of the Study Group as an ongoing entity that could influence the implementation of its recommendations, the coordinator was unable to operationalize the plan smoothly. Also, it afforded other existing units in the hospital an opportunity to strengthen their requests for additional resource support during a time of declining resources. Consequently, the health promotion program was not fully stabilized during its initial year of operation. By switching roles from primarily collaborative problem-solving processors to expert technical assistants, we were not in an advantageous position to facilitate the stabilization of the programmatic directions in health promotion. Because our primary contact at the hospital was the interim coordinator, our exposure to other Study Group members was limited. The Group's absence at this stage prevented a unified, coordinated implementation of all recommendations along with the establishment of an ongoing base for sustained development activity.

Termination. The final subphase of termination proceeded rather smoothly. Ideally, prior to terminating the consultant-consultee relationship, the consultant should have an opportunity to assess the consultee's readiness to terminate, solicit feedback on the consultant's effectiveness, develop a structure for ongoing support to the consultee (if warranted),

and schedule a post-follow-up session to review progress on the imple
mented changes.

We had a specified completion date in each of our written agreements.
Obviously, the consultee was not ready to terminate at the end of the firs
agreement as evidenced by the invitation for us to continue from the Chie
Executive Officer. However, at the completion of our second agreement
there was prior discussion of the consultee's readiness to terminate. It was
their belief that they were ready to terminate the consultant relationship
and expand the duties of the interim coordinator. Consequently, we began
preparations for our departure.

We met, on our own time, with a representative selection of management and Study Group members to solicit feedback on our performance
We also invited the interim coordinator to contact us for clarification or
any follow-up issues or for additional support if necessary. He accepted
our invitation and made several follow-up contacts for information and
support. Although we suggested a follow-up meeting to review progress
a meeting for this purpose was never scheduled. While we were somewha
concerned about the lack of a meeting, he assured us that our assistance
had produced positive results for the hospital. Moreover, while a full-time
director was not hired, all of our remaining recommendations were
followed. Thus, while there was some consternation on our part, our overall assessment concluded that the consultation was a success. This was
confirmed over time with reports from other local health care officials
that programmatic efforts by the hospital were proceeding.

Issues in Retrospect

Throughout the course of our engagement we were thrust into a number
of situations that created demands above those posed by our collaborative
problem-solving, and planning role. In response, we had to perform se-
lectively in advocacy roles and as technical experts. While these two
functions were clearly subordinate to our dominant activity, it is useful to
describe several illustrative events because they help capture the richness
of our experience and present a very realistic picture of the role conflicts
and resulting serious consequences that consultants frequently confront.

Advocacy Role

Our advocacy roles centered about senior administration's desire to use
our involvement in a manner that could help influence medical staff and

Board of Trustees actions to advance the health promotion initiative. Not every attempt at advocacy was successful, however. For example, at a fairly early stage in the project, the Study Group felt compelled to begin signaling its seriousness by implementing simple actions that would heighten awareness of its functions. One of these involved removal of all cigarette machines from the hospital. Recognizing that the medical staff had vested interests in suppressing large-scale health promotion program development, senior administration positioned this recommendation so that it was very closely associated with us. A small number of influential physicians became aware of this possibility, voiced their objection to the administration, and the proposal was withdrawn. This action created an unnecessary level of anxiety among several of the Study Group members as well as ourselves. That it happened so quickly reminded us to be vary careful not to create a level of enthusiasm so great that the defeat of politically unpopular proposals (by certain constituencies) could derail an entire effort. In retrospect, we would have more carefully channeled this early enthusiasm into our intended plan. However, we were taken somewhat by surprise at the speed with which this proposal was advanced. And still being unfamiliar with the political culture of the institution, we realistically had no way to prevent it. During our own private discussions we thought it very likely that certain senior administrators were conducting an early test of potential political reactions to the longer term effort. In addition, we believed they expected us to lobby extensively for this early change and achieve success through the use of our credibility as technical experts. Nevertheless, the experience forced us to be more deliberate with the Study Group, and gave us reason to stimulate internal debate within the group itself so that potentially adverse reactions to future recommendations could be anticipated and managed more effectively.

While the above example focuses on a single event, advocacy can also require a substantial time commitment by consultants and extend throughout the entire engagement. In our case it became necessary to forge an extremely close working relationship with the chairman of the Health Promotion Study Group in order to achieve two objectives. The first was ensuring that the Chairman fully understood the nature of the planning effort so that he or she could in turn influence key Board of Trustee members and medical staff physicians for support of the Study Group's recommendations. In principle, we do not believe that this type of activity is unreasonable. As consultants whose professional values supported the underlying assumptions about the effectiveness of health promotion, we felt that we had a significant stake in the outcome of the Study Group

effort. Thus our efforts to ensure that the chief spokesperson of the grou
could present a justifiable case to hospital decision makers were wa
ranted. We shared these values with senior administration and did not be
lieve our work with the Study Group Chairman was unreasonably partisa

The second objective (although never made explicit) of our relationsh
with the Study Group Chairman involved senior administration desires
placate him in order to obtain support for a number of other planned i
itiatives. By appointing him as Chairman of the Study Group, senior a
ministration believed that voting positions at the Board level wou
reflect its own interests. Obviously, our role in fulfilling these objectiv
extended beyond advocacy and involved co-optation. Although we we
quite uncomfortable with this arrangement, it was necessary in order
ensure that our partisan efforts in effecting systemic change within tl
hospital were successful.

Our advocacy efforts with the Study Group Chairman generally i
volved meetings that occurred outside of the formal deliberations of th
body. There were thus two channels of activity, and two correspondir
consultant roles, being undertaken in parallel. The first was the collab
rative, problem-solving, and planning effort that was undertaken in tl
public sessions with the study Group. The second involved numero
private sessions with its Chairman.

Finally, we were subjected to occasional efforts by certain Study Grou
members to gain our support in order to advance their own parochi
objectives. One effort involved a department manager who was attemp
ing to increase her support base within the hospital. Accordingly, th
manager made numerous attempts in private to influence our recomme
dations in a manner that supported her personal objectives. This type
lobbying activity can be fairly common and is usually manageable. In o
case we had protected ourselves in the first Study Group session b
gaining consensus on procedural rules that stipulated that only issues
group interest, and not those of a personal nature, could be addressed
the planning process. Thus the collaborative model involving the Grou
offered some insulation from individual attempts to secure us as advocat
for causes that could not be discussed publicly.

Technical Expert and Assistance Role

Forces within the competitive environment were mainly responsible f
our functioning as technical experts. As noted earlier in the case discu
sion, the client's rivalry with one competing hospital in its service are

created frequent demands for increased speed in the conduct of our activities. Our preference, given the collaborative nature of the relationship with the Study Group, was for a more deliberate pace. However, we also recognized that senior administration had to contend with a very real threat from the other facility. In addition, its credibility (and ours as well) would have been severely damaged if the other hospital had entered the health promotion arena first and established a dominant position within the community. As a result we had to balance both needs. In general, we accomplished this by providing structure to the Study Group in order to focus its efforts quickly at various stages in the planning process. This was accomplished during the market analysis (where we helped design the three assessments) as well as in the identification of health promotion program options. In both cases delay could have been substantial enough for our client to lose a possible competitive advantage. And these situations illustrate the need for consultants to shift roles voluntarily, sometimes away from their dominant value system, in order to assist the client more fully.

At the conclusion of our engagement (during the stabilization and termination subphases) we shifted to a dominant technical assistance role. While we consented to this shift, we now believe that it was caused by two factors. The first was an overestimation by the new CEO of the client's ability to assume complete direction of the program. The second contributing factor was our own desire to cooperate with the new CEO. In this case, we do not believe that the result was favorable, and stronger adherence to our collaborative model would undoubtedly have helped our client through the last critical subphases of the engagement.

Personal Reflections

The consulting experience left us with several distinct impressions about future consultations. We will review those impressions within the context of the subphases that we employed during this case.

Entry into this consulting relationship occurred very smoothly. We believe that this relative ease of entry was fostered by the early explanation of our consultation style and our expectations for the consulting experience. We purposely did not rush this process in order to be certain that we had gathered several different views of the problem situation and the anticipated consultant role. Also, during this time we established the groundwork for a healthy relationship.

The *relationship* subphase, in our opinion, is one of the two most critical stages. If the proper tone is not established early in the relationship (i.e., open, honest) and if an accurate initial assessment of the problem is not made, it is difficult and very time consuming to make a recovery. Consequently, it is our recommendation that consultants allow sufficient time for relationship development to occur. Also, we believe that consultants must model the desired characteristics of the consultant-consultee relationship. In our experience, the appropriate use of naturally occurring humor has been an effective tool in establishing a warm, friendly, and relaxed atmosphere.

The *assessment* subphase is dependent on a sound identification of essential and desired data that are necessary for resolution of the consulting issue. We devoted a significant amount of time to the design of this data collection system. However, we were constantly conscious of the fact that our perceived needs of essential data were not necessarily the same as those of the consultee. Thus we maintained close contact with the consultee as we were formulating the recommendations for the data collection plan. Also, we found it helpful to blend data identification systems from different disciplines. For example, in this case we blended a health promotion model with a marketing model. The end result was a richer, more complete data set from which to derive recommendations for program direction. Because of the complexity of the process and the relative lack of familiarity with this type of system, it was necessary to train the subcommittee members before they embarked on their task.

Planning and preparing for change was a very interactive and collaborative process. We used a variety of group communication techniques to facilitate this process. At times, as a consulting team, it was necessary to check one another when one of us sensed that the other was developing ownership of a recommendation. This served as a distinct example of one of the benefits to be derived from working as a member of a consulting team.

During the development of the *implementation strategy* and *evaluation* subphases two events occurred that produced a profound effect on our consulting experience. The first was the appointment of a new Chief Executive Officer. This unanticipated event affected the team-building process in which we had engaged the Study Group and subcommittees from the inception of our relationship. All of the issues that are confronted in the inclusion of a new group member were magnified by the position of influence that she held in the organization. In retrospect, we would have backtracked and taken time to reconfirm the recommendations of the Study Group with the new Chief Executive Officer before proceeding to the Board of Trustees. We believe this would have increased the CEO's ownership of the recommendations and influenced the allocation of resources to the program for ongoing development.

The second event that had a pronounced effect was our decision to switch roles from a dominant process, collaborator role to a dominant technical assistance role. This decision removed us from a position wherein we could more effectively enable the *stabilization* of the health promotion program. Because we were working with a written agreement we felt obligated to honor our prescribed role and not interfere with the internal operations of the hospital. As a result, we both experienced a frustration that we had not fully facilitated our original task. Intellectually, we know that ownership and direction of the program is the domain of the consultee. However, that knowledge does not eliminate feelings that consultants may experience. We believe that we would have been more effective had we not consented to a shift in our role.

At the time of *termination* we had done all that we had agreed to do and the hospital was eager to manage the program with its internal resources. Consequently it was not a difficult process to disengage and provide the follow-up services that were of mutual agreement.

This consulting relationship serves as a practical example of a collaborative process model that was effective in fulfilling its original intent, the design of a plan for a health promotion program. At the same time, this case demonstrates that shifts in consultant role may be accompanied by internal conflicts that must be resolved in order to avoid a conflict of interest or to avoid a disempowerment of the consultee. We believe that the presence of two consultants in this situation enabled each consultant to be more conscious of, and resolve, conflicts as they emerged.

Implications for Training

The diverse nature of the demands presented in this case, as well as in our other consultations, pose significant challenges to any academic program that attempts to forge a closer link between training and practice. One of the obvious challenges is ensuring that consultants are psychologically and technically prepared to shift roles in order to fulfill the objectives of the engagement. While our dominant role in this case was cyclical and collaborative, we executed a significant shift at the end of our engagement in order to address the expectations of our client. Moreover at various times throughout the engagement, we were forced to perform in multiple roles simultaneously so that the development, advocacy, and technical needs of our consultees could be met in a manner that did not disrupt the natural flow of events. This required a great deal of flexibility on our part and is consistent with the demands placed on us in our other long-term, organizational consultations.

Likewise, the intellectual demands placed on us were diverse, and multidisciplinary. For example, at different stages in the consultation we had to master the skills associated with collaborative planning models (i.e., group decision making, brainstorming, interviewing, and observation), technical advisement in health promotion program development and training and staff development. Quite often, consultant credibility and effectiveness were dependent on our facility with many different subjects and the speed with which we could adapt to changing intellectual requirements. This again coincides with our experiences in other settings.

Finally, we also had to employ a sensitivity to the sociopolitical culture of our client organization, and have the "street sense" to maneuver effectively within a dynamic and fragmented hospital system. The demands here transcended purely intellectual and theoretical considerations, and forced us to be very introspective about our basic personal and professional ethics as we deliberated over how we should respond to client expectations that were not made clear during the early stages of our project. Where conflicting ethical demands appear suddenly and unexpectedly, and when responses must be immediate, theoretical prescriptions can prove sophomoric. They will provide little help to the consultant who is unprepared for the harsh reality of organizational politics, and who has never been forced to trade off one deeply held value for another. When long-term, system-wide organizational change is sought, sociopolitical demands appear to be inevitable. Therefore, we believe training in consultation must accept sociopolitical realities and include a certain amount of "seasoning" to ensure adequate preparation of students.

Academic training for consultation can first be directed toward broadening specific skills that develop practitioner versatility. While we embrace the dominant human-development value system (and believe warrants substantial attention in training programs) the relevance of information and technical expertise, and advocacy roles cannot be overlooked. Thus the competencies required for effective performance of all three roles must be openly accepted and addressed. Didactic instruction, simulation exercises, and instructor supervision are only three training modalities that have merit. In addition, however, the development of professional judgment that can determine when one specific role should be performed at the expense of others is perhaps even more important. This subject is addressed below.

Second, given the systemic nature of organizational issues, training in consultation must pursue the development of broad-based understandings of problems. Because many of our schools currently have a more narrow, functional (or professional) orientation, training programs should seek a synthesis that reverses our inclination toward specialization. For example, theoretical prescriptions from a variety of relevant disciplines should be integrated in didactic instruction. This will allow trainees to become sensitive to the underlying assumptions and value systems of the different professions that are frequently brought together in any organizational setting. Similarly, relevant content knowledge from a variety of disciplines should be integrated. Given the limited opportunities for pursuing course work in several disciplines, it may be possible to bring together students (in project teams) with different academic backgrounds who share a common professional interest in consultation. Both of these proposals warrant further exploration even though they run counter to American academic tradition, which is oriented to specialization. However, other nations have proved successful in synthesizing different disciplines. In West Germany, for example, excellent apprenticeship programs provide workers with a generalist orientation. In addition, Japanese engineers are required to be extremely knowledgeable not only about their own jobs, but also those of others with whom they work in corporations. This has helped reinforce the cross-functional nature of problem solving and allowed them to achieve a superior international position in manufacturing.

Finally, training in consultation must include increased opportunities for field-based experiences. These should focus not only on the application and refinement of specific skills, but perhaps more importantly on the enhancement of professional judgment, the development of organizational savvy, and an increased understanding of the sociopolitical realities of planning and decision making in organizations. While university supervision and quality control will be required in order to ensure the value of such experiences, an equally critical variable will be the availability of on-site direction of trainees. Not only must sponsors of these experiences have a demonstrated commitment to the training requirements, but they must also be willing to tolerate trainees' mistakes, spend a great deal of time mentoring, and occasionally trade off optimum results for the opportunity to participate in the training activity. Although the magnitude of this challenge must be acknowledged, the long-term effectiveness of professionals in consultation is clearly at stake.

References

Bader, B. (1982). *Planning hospital health promotion services for business and industry.* Chicago: American Hospital Association.

Bills, S. (Ed). (1982). Hospital learns the hard way how not to design programs for business and industry. *Promoting Health, 3,* 1-3.

Blocher, D. (1975). A systematic eclectic approach to consultation. In C. Parker (Ed.), *Psychological consultations: Helping teachers meet special needs.* Minneapolis: Leadership Training Institute.

Bosch, S. (1981). A nationwide business opportunity for hospitals. *Michigan Hospitals, 2,* 12-13.

Brokes, A. (1975). A process model of consultation. In C. Parker (Ed.), *Psychological consultation: Helping teachers meet special needs* (pp. 185-203). Minneapolis: Leadership Training Institute.

Burrow, E., & Smith, M. (1961, September). Hospital develops occupational health service for local industries. *Hospitals, 16,* 145-151.

Caplan, G. (1970). *Theory and practice of mental health consultation.* New York: Basic Books.

Carlson, J. (1975). Consulting: Facilitating school change. *Elementary School Guidance and Counseling, 7,* 83-88.

Gallessich, I. (1985). Toward a meta-theory of consultation. In D. Brown & D. Kurpius (Eds.), Consultation [Special issue], The Counseling Psychologist, 13, 336-354.

Green, L., Kreuter, M., Deeds, S., & Partridge, K. (1980). *Health education planning: A diagnostic approach.* Palo Alto, CA: Mayfield.

Havelock, R. (1973). *The change agent's guide to innovation in education.* Englewood Cliffs, NJ: Education Technology Publication.

Herzlinger, R. (1989, March-April). The failed revolution in health care—The role of management. *Harvard Business Review,* pp. 95-103.

Lippitt, R., Watson, J., & Westley, B. (1958). *The dynamics of planned change.* New York: Harcourt, Brace & World.

Opatz, J. (Ed.). (1987). *Health promotion evaluation: Measuring the organizational impact.* Stevens Point, WI: National Wellness Institute.

Simon, S., Howe, L., & Kirschenbaum, H. (1972). *Values clarification: A handbook of practical strategies for teachers and students.* New York: Hart.

U.S. Department of Health, Education and Welfare. (1979). *Healthy people: The Surgeon General's report on health promotion and disease prevention.* Washington, DC: Government Printing Office.

U.S. House of Representatives. (1981). *National healthcare reform act of 1981 (H.R. 850).* Washington, DC: Government Printing Office.

Wagner, D. (1976, September). *A consultative model for the development of health policy.* Paper presented at the meeting of the International Union for Health Education, Ottawa, Canada.

Yenney, S. (1981). Wellness care. *Michigan Hospitals, 2,* 5-6.

6

Reducing Racism and Sexism in a University Setting Through Organizational Consultation

JAMES M. O'NEIL

ROBERT K. CONYNE

R ACISM and sexism are personal and institutional forms of oppression that victimize millions of Americans in our society every year. Attention to racism and sexism peaked in the early 1970s, but in the 1980s the destructive outcomes of these forms of discrimination were either minimized or ignored. Affirmative action plans and hiring quotas were abolished in the early 1980s and recent Supreme Court cases suggest a more conservative interpretation of how racism-sexism oppress individuals. Racism and sexism are important issues to be addressed in the 1990s, as witnessed by the frequent reports of racial and sexual violence in the media.

Racism and sexism have their roots in our political, social, and economic growth as a culture. Sex and racial discrimination demonstrate people's difficulty accepting individual differences and our inability to accept racial, sexual, and gender role differences without insulting, abusing, or violating each other. Reducing the causes and effects of racism-sexism is a primary challenge for psychologists committed to equality, justice, and human dignity among people. The high human stakes involved with racism and sexism have made these persisting problems prime targets for psychologists and other mental health workers.

This chapter describes a three-year consultation in the late 1970s focused on reducing institutional racism/sexism at a large university. The first author chaired the Campus Committee to Reduce Sex and Race Role Stereotypes. The university administration asked the committee to enumerate recommendations that could reduce sex and race role stereotypes on campus. Eighteen months of consultation focused on making the recommendations publicly visible to insure their implementation. The second author served as an outside and expert analyzer of this consultation process.

This chapter provides a detailed analysis of the consultation dynamics. The cyclical, collaborative problem-solving processes that occurred between the consultant and the consultee are emphasized. Numerous concepts, theories, and approaches have been used to describe and analyze the dynamics of this organizational consultation. From these, three major theoretical perspectives have been incorporated into the case study: (a) Gallessich's (1985) metatheories of human-development and social/political consultation; (b) Conoley and Conoley's (1982) advocacy and process consultation conceptualizations; (c) Lippitt and Lippitt's (1986) consultation phases and roles. In accordance with the overall plan of this book, the chapter first presents the background information providing a context for the complexity of the consultation process. Next, the consultation plan and implementation are described using Lippitt and Lippitt's phases of consultation. These phases demonstrate how the consultant and consultee used a collaborative problem-solving approach in identifying the problem, generating solutions, recycling feedback, and evaluating the effectiveness of the consultation over time. Next, the evaluation of the consultation is reported as well as the analysis of the multiple roles used in the consultation. Finally, the consultant's personal reflections and recommendations for training future consultants are given.

Consultation Background

The consultation background includes specific demographic information on the university's organization, characteristics, and administrative arrangements. The many individuals, groups, and governing bodies that were affected by the consultation are described. Also, the ecological context of the consultation is given by describing the city, campus community, and certain historical events that preceded the consultation process. Finally, the preconsultation background is described, including the specific events leading to the 18 months of consultation with the university administration.

Demographic Information

University Characteristics. This state-supported institution was a major center of learning and enrolled more than 20,000 students each year. It was located in a small city of 50,000 and had conferred degrees for over 100 years. The university offered more than 90 undergraduate majors and more than 70 graduate majors, programs, or fields of study. It was recognized as a major academic institution and recognized nationally as a major center for its teaching, research, and service.

Student-Faculty Characteristics. The students and faculty were primarily white and middle class. Seventy percent of the undergraduate students were in-state residents and 60% of the graduate students were out-of-state residents. The sex ratio of undergraduate students was 49% male and 51% female. Graduate student enrollment was 60% male and 40% female.

Institution's Administrative Arrangement. The university was headed by a president and executive vice president along with vice presidents for Academic Affairs, Student Affairs, and Graduate Study. Faculty legislative bodies included the university's elected Senate Committee and the American Association of University Professors (AAUP). There was no union and the university funding came from legislative allocation, alumni support, and student tuition fees.

Participants, Groups, Consultation Parties. Figure 6.1 is a pictorial representation of the major parties involved in the consultation between September, 1977 and August, 1980. The solid lines between individuals or groups indicate formalized relationships between and among the parties. The dotted lines represent informal relationships that evolved because of the institutional dynamics. Each major party in Figure 6.1 is defined below and referred to in subsequent sections of the chapter.

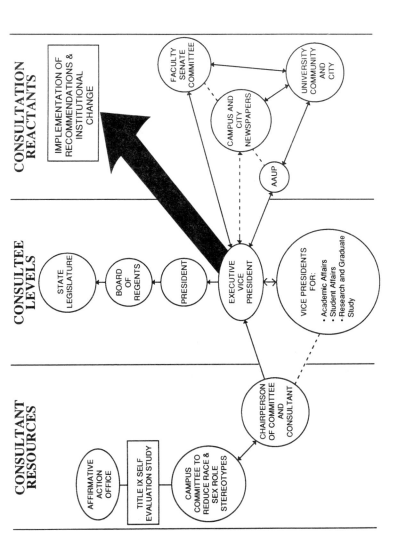

Figure 6.1. Consultation Parties, Groups, and Participants

The center of Figure 6.1 shows the consultee levels. It depicts the direct relationship existing among the state legislature, board of regents, president, executive vice president, and the three vice presidents. These relationships represented the governing bodies and the institutional structures of the University. The Executive Vice President was the primary consultee and was responsible for the day-to-day running of the university. The three vice presidents were secondary consultees and deliberated on ways to implement the committee's recommendations.

The left side of Figure 6.1 includes the consultant resources. These resources were concerned with developing policy to eradicate sexism and racism. Each resource was involved directly with the university administration. The Affirmative Action Office was responsible for generating the Title IX Self Evaluation Study required by the federal government's Department of Health, Education and Welfare (HEW). The Campus Committee To Reduce Race and Sex Role Stereotypes was formed by the University administration to specify ways to implement the Title IX Self Evaluation Study results pertaining to race and sex discrimination. The chairperson of that committee was the primary consultant. He directed the committee and led the consultation efforts after the committee work had been completed. The chairperson was a trained counseling psychologist and was an untenured assistant professor who held appointments both in the University Counseling Center and the APA-approved Counseling Psychology Program.

The right side of Figure 6.1 includes the consultation reactants, that is, those parties who responded to the consultation and committee's report. The reactants included the University's Faculty Senate Committee and a subcommittee of the American Association of University Professors (AAUP). As well, both the university and city newspapers were involved in reporting the events that occurred during the consultation activities.

Ecological Context of the Consultation

Historical events of the city and campus community prior to the consultation provide important background to understand the consultation dynamics. First, the city was a moderately progressive community in a somewhat conservative state. It was greatly influenced by the fluid and progressive atmosphere of the university community. In the early 1970s the city and university were centers for political unrest, social activism,

Vietnam War protests, racial conflict, and challenges to the status quo. Bill Moyers wrote in his book, *Listen To America,* that:

> This community has in recent years experienced open conflict between blacks and whites, arson, student violence and death. The town is large enough to harbor several communities with their own way of life. It is small enough for every citizen to feel the impact of colliding values. The people I met looked at events through the lens of their own personal experience and defined truth by what they saw. So fiercely had each adherent sworn loyalty to his part of the whole, that the idea of community—of a place where people exist competitively without malice—would been hard to repair. (Moyers, 1971, p. 122)

Steps were initiated to resolve these social problems in the early 1970s. The city formed a steering committee that arranged for external consultation to provide workshops to assess and promote constructive change. Auerback (1973) reported that these workshops produced 80 suggestions to improve community relations. These recommendations included establishing a day-care center, hiring more human-relations staff, improving police-community relations, involving the schools more in the community, and improving relations between blacks and whites. The community had experienced serious racial and political problems and it had committed itself to constructive community action.

Even with these progressive activities implemented, the community and the university were highly sensitive to political and social issues (e.g., racism) that might produce further disruption, conflict, or "bad press" throughout the rest of the state. For example, the state legislature in 1971 voted very marginal pay increases for faculty, at least partially because of the political-social unrest on campus during that year. The low salary increases were a message to university administrators that they should maintain order on campus and keep the university focused on the educational rather the political-social issues of the day. The social unrest of the early 1970s had produced sensitivities and defensiveness that made the issues of institutional racism/sexism difficult topics for discussion, change, and consultation.

Preconsultation Background

In the fall of 1976, the university completed a self-evaluation study to determine whether it was in compliance with the requirements of Title IX of the Higher Education Amendment of 1972 (*Title IX,* 1972). A self-evaluation committee was directed by the Affirmative Action Office. The committee reviewed the university's policies and practices to determine whether the university was in compliance with laws that prohibited discrimination based on sex, race, or other areas. The committee focused particularly on the area of admissions, treatment of students, and employment. The self-evaluation committee forwarded a 100 page Title IX Self Evaluation Report to the Executive Vice President, emphasizing potential areas of discrimination. One recommendation suggested that a new committee be created to make recommendations on how to reduce the effect of race and sex role stereotypes on campus.

In September 1977, the Executive Vice President appointed a committee to enumerate recommendations to reduce race and sex role stereotypes at the university. The committee's charge was to generate solutions to the problems of sex and race role stereotyping at the University. The committee was named The Campus Committee to Reduce Race and Sex Role Stereotypes. Eleven professionals were invited to participate on the committee including: four faculty members, four student personnel workers, two students (one undergraduate and one graduate student), and one representative of the central administration. The sex and race background of the committee members included seven males, four females; three blacks, and eight whites. The committee's functioning over a nine-month period represented the preconsultation background of this case study.

The first author was elected chairperson and directed the 11-member committee. The committee met nine times from October 13, 1977 to June 21, 1978. The committee process included a number of specific steps. First, all members of the committee reviewed the confidential Title IX Self Evaluation Report. This review stimulated questions about the specific goals and objectives for the committee. The Executive Vice President then met with the committee to clarify the committee's task. Following this meeting, it was recommended that subcommittees study specific parts of the Title IX Self Evaluation Report and make concrete recommendations to the larger committee. The four subcommittees included: (a) Admissions and Recruitment, (b) Treatment of Students, (c) Career Development and Counseling, (d) Faculty and Staff Employment.

Each subcommittee wrote mini-reports that were circulated to other subcommittees and discussed between January 16, 1978 and March 1, 1978. These subcommittee reports included a list of specific and important recommendations. The chairperson then wrote a final report that was critiqued by the entire committee. On May 15, 1978 the final draft was approved by the committee.

The resulting report, *Recommendations for Reducing Race and Sex Role Stereotyping,* was sent with a cover letter to the Executive Vice President of the University on June 21, 1978. The 27-page report specified 53 recommendations to reduce sexism and racism on the campus. The 53 recommendations were clustered into the following seven areas: (a) Admissions and Recruitment of Students; (b) Career Development, Counseling, and Resource Development; (c) Faculty and Staff Employment; (d) Sensitization, In-Service, Educational Programming Needs for the Campus; (e) Treatment of Students; (f) Academic Support Services and Developmental Assistance for Students; and (g) Identification of Data and Research.

On July 10, 1978 the Executive Vice President sent a memo thanking the committee and indicating that the report would be discussed at the administrative retreat to be held by the President and all vice presidents of the university. While most committee members ceased active functioning following submittal of the recommendations, important consultation continued. After submitting the final report, the first author consulted with the Executive Vice President and other university administrators over 18 months on how to implement the recommendations. This case study focuses on the consultation that occurred during those 18 months.

Consultation Issues, Plan, and Theoretical Approaches

Implementation strategies focused on the consultation issue of operationalizing the committee's recommendations. These strategies implied receiving explicit public statements from the university administration that specific recommendations would be studied, assigned, and implemented in the university community. An explicit consultation contract between the consultant and the multiple university consultees was impossible to develop because of the volatile nature of the issues and personalities involved. Yet, an informal agreement developed between the consultant and the consultee (Executive Vice President) that allowed the consultation relationship to evolve and work. The consultant's primary role with the Executive Vice President and other administrators was a collegial, consultative, and collaborative problem-solving approach focused on the issues of racism and sexism on campus.

Much of the consultation plan over the 18 months of the project emerge
from the quickly changing events of institutional life. A contingency ap
proach to both the interpersonal and institutional dynamics emerged
allowing a variety of consultation roles and interventions to be matche
with the evolving situation. These roles and interventions are delineate
in detail later in the chapter.

The consultant approached the consultation using published rationale
from the literature on counselors as social change agents (Conyne, 1977)
environmental assessment specialists (Conyne, 1975; Conyne et al., 1978)
prevention experts (Albee & Joffe, 1977), and consultants (Conyne &
Clack, 1975; Hamilton & Meade, 1979; Leonard, 1977). At this time, th
literature on campus consultation was still emerging but the roles an
functions of the consultant had been articulated in the literature. The con
sultant had recently graduated from his doctoral program and indirect
preventive, and consultative interventions had been studied, emphasized
and experimented with during his training.

In this retrospective analysis, we have found two sets of ideologies t
be very useful in defining the consultation process. First, Gallessich's (1985
metatheories of social/political and human-development consultation re
flect the consultant's goals and process. Second, Conoley and Conoley'
(1986) descriptions of process and advocacy consultation help describ
the consultation dynamics and events. Gallessich's human-developmen
consultation and Conoley and Conoley's process consultation are com
bined in this analysis to demonstrate one unified approach to consultation
At a secondary level, Gallessich's social/political consultation and Con
oley and Conoley's advocacy consultation share similar premises tha
guided the consultation process.

Common values are implied in human-development and process con
sultation. Human-development consultation is focused on improving work
ing and learning environments and process consultation uses social
psychological theory to help consultees become more aware of transaction
that affect their productivity and work. Both consultation approaches sug
gest that a collaborative problem-solving approach develops between th
consultant and consultee. Collaborative problem solving implies that th
consultant and consultee mutually move through a series of steps to iden
tify the problem, generate solutions, evaluate the effectiveness of the so
lution, and recycle feedback as appropriate. As will be observed later i

the case study, there were some identifiable steps (i.e., phases) in the consultation, and information was recycled regularly. Human-development consultation and process consultation are process oriented and directed toward developing specific solutions to problems through educational and facilitative roles.

Process and human-development consultation accurately describe the process employed in this intervention. The campus committee and the consultant were responsible for assessing the university environment and recommending ways to reduce racism and sexism on campus. The consultant then worked collaboratively with the university administration to evolve specific solutions to the problems of racism and sexism on the campus.

Advocacy and social/political consultation also describe aspects of the consultation in this case (Conoley & Conoley, 1986; Gallessich, 1985). Both involve consultation actions designed to improve basic social and political issues, processes, and structures. Racism and sexism were social-political issues that seriously affected the entire organizational system of the university. In both advocacy and social and political consultation the consultant's roles and position are unique. Advocacy consultants ally themselves with an underpowered group and enact a set of political values. In a similar fashion, social/political consultants are partisans and confront systems that are not living up to their stated values. Advocacy consultants use power, influence, and political processes to influence people and systems. They seek to organize people, publicize events, and use data, negotiations, and confrontations to produce change. Both advocacy and social/political consultation contributed to the consultation reported in this case, which was aimed at reducing institutional racism and sexism.

Consultation Implementation

The complete consultation is described in detail in Table 6.1. This table depicts 23 activities mapping the entire consultation process, including the follow-up evaluations.

The consultation dynamics and activities listed in Table 6.1 are detailed below using Lippitt and Lippitt's (1986) phases of consultation.

Text continued on p. 159

TABLE 6.1 Consultation Phases, Activities, and Interventions

Year-Month	Consultation Phases	Activities & Interventions
1978 June	I & II	1. Twenty-eight page report submitted enumerating 53 recommendations to reduce sex and race role stereotyping. Seven major areas of concern that the report made recommendations are: (1) Admissions & Recruitment; (2) Career Development, Counseling & Resource Development; (3) Sensitization, In-service, Educational Programming needs for the campus; (4) Academic support services & developmental assistance for students; (5) Faculty & Staff employment; (6) Identification of data & research. Cover letter written encouraging dialogue and action.
July	I & II	2. Memo thanking committee for their work was sent from the Executive Vice President. Memo indicates the report will be shared with the President, other Vice Presidents, Council of Deans, and Personnel in the Division of Student Affairs. The report was placed on Joint Administrative Council's Retreat Agenda for consideration.
September- October	III	3. Meeting time and agenda set by chairperson for committee and Vice President to meet. Goals of meeting were to: (1) obtain reactions to our report from Vice President, (2) discuss next steps toward assignment of tasks and implementations of the recommendations, (3) ascertain whether the 53 recommendations are budgetary priorities for the University.
November	IV & V	4. Committee meets with Vice Presidents to discuss recommendations. Vice Presidents request that 53 recommendations be priortized in terms of those needing: (1) immediate attention, (2) immediate budgetary attention.
		5. Chairperson meets with Executive Vice President to discuss prioritizing process. It was decided that committee members' rankings of the recommendations would be ready for a January, 1979 meeting.
December	IV & V	6. Committee members receive and fill out questionnaire ranking 53 recommendations in terms of those needing immediate attention and budgetary support.
		7. Chairperson calculates and communicates the priority recommendations to the Executive Vice President. Overall, the rankings included 20 recommendations needing immediate attention and implementation and 15 recommendations specified as needing immediate budgetary support. Cover letter encouraged implementation.

TABLE 6.1 Continued

Year-Month	Consultation Phases	Activities & Interventions
		8. Executive Vice President acknowledges that the prioritized recommendations have been received and will place the recommendations of the committee on the agenda of early January administrative retreat.
1979 January	IV & V	9. Committee meets with Vice Presidents to analyze the rankings, decide on budget, and next steps toward implementation. Budget requests denied. Status of recommendations unclear and next steps unclear.
March	IV & V	10. Chairperson of committee met individually with Vice President for Student Affairs, Vice President for Academic Affairs, Vice President for Graduate Studies and Executive Vice President to ascertain their opinions about the report and next steps.
April	IV & V	11. Chairperson writes memo to Executive Vice President specifying 15 recommendations that could be implemented without great cost. Memo indicates: (1) the target population served, (2) the offices and personnel involved in implementation. The memo mentions the importance of administrative support for the recommendation if any action is to come from the committee's work. Also, it is stated that all recommendations are directed at: (1) improving our institutional operations, (2) retaining and attracting students, (3) reviewing and solidifying our commitments to educational equity for all races and sexes, (4) eliminating both personal and institutional forms of racism/sexism at the University.
April-May	IV & V	12. Meetings with campus groups and individuals to discuss the status of the recommendations.
June	IV & V	13. Executive Vice President forwards 15 recommendations, target populations, potential personnel involved in implementation to all Vice Presidents. The memo encourages them to review it and to have it be an agenda item in their late Summer or early Fall retreat.
July	IV & V	14. AAUP Chapter discusses the status of the committee's report and question why there had been no action. AAUP had requested a copy of the report which was sent by the Executive Vice Presidents. Newspaper report of these events appeared in the city newspaper.

TABLE 6.1 Continued

Year-Month	Consultation Phases	Activities & Interventions
September	IV & V	15. Senate Committee discussed the recommendations and delay action. Criticism of the report from members of this legislative body indicated the report was inadequate, provocative, muddled, poorly written, and an unfortunate document. Other members felt the Affirmative Action should satisfy University's commitment to prevent sex and race role stereotyping and not have "redundant" actions by committee. The University newspaper reported the Senate Committee's consideration and criticism of the report.
October	IV & V	16. Central Administration discuss the 15 recommendations with representative of SenEx and AAUP. The University newspaper reported these events and printed the recommendation as part of their reporting. Chairperson responds to criticism and makes comments about the status of the recommendations.
	IV & V	17. Chairperson writes a chronological history of the consultation and disseminates it to the local media and Executive Vice President.
December	IV & V	18. Executive Vice President communicates to Chairperson Vice Presidents, Chair of Senate Committee, and public media that 11 of the 15 recommendations would be implemented by various administrative personnel. An eight page report specified which recommendations would be implemented and the rationale for the actions. The University and city newspaper report front page stories on the recommendations. Chairperson and Executive Vice President are interviewed in the story about the process, status, and results of the committee's work.
1980 July	VI	19. Chairperson provides Executive Vice President with name and vita of outside consultant to provide advice about how to more effectively recruit and retain black (or other non-white) faculty and staff at the University (Recommendation 12).
1981 April	VI	20. Follow-up of the effect of recommendations is started by consulting with Vice President for Student Affairs. He provide a list of outcomes that he has observed and particular personnel to be interviewed.

TABLE 6.1 Continued

Year-Month	Consultation Phases	Activities & Interventions
June	VI	21. Follow-up is approved by Executive Vice President who is now the Acting President. The University Attorney evaluates the follow-up questions and asks that one be omitted. The Acting President writes a letter of support for the follow-up study that is attached to questionnaire.
July	VI	22. Follow-up memo and questions are sent to 50 professionals asking them to respond to four questions about their perception of the effects of the recommendations.
1982 July	VI	23. Personal interview with Executive Vice President is conducted to obtain his reaction to the consultation 34 months after implementation of recommendations.

Consultation Phase I and II:
Entry, Formulating a Contract, and
Establishing a Helping Relationship (Activities 1 & 2)

Entry to the consultation occurred when the Executive Vice President formed the committee and asked for recommendations to reduce race and sex role stereotypes. After the final report was submitted, an informal contract was established. The final committee discussions centered on how to hold subsequent discussions with the Executive Vice President and his vice presidents about implementing the recommendations. These discussions provided a basis for an informal contract between the consultant and consultee.

The cover letter and introduction to the final report outlined the committee's philosophy, goals, and desire for dialogue about how to implement the recommendations. The following verbatim quotations from the cover letter demonstrate the premises used to make the transition from the committee work to active consultation (see particularly the last sentence):

Readers need to be sensitive to how sexism/racism are subtly and fully integrated into the social, historical, and political and educational practices of our country, and therefore the university. Sexism and racism are part of our institutional policy, not necessarily because of our intent, but because of the social, political, economic, and historical events that are part of our nation's history. The recommendations are based on numerous documents including university, state, federal laws that prohibit discrimination base on race, color, religion, national origin, sex, age, disability, or political affiliations in its educational programs, activities, and policies. Progress in decreasing racism/sexism will not take place without budgetary support to implement the 53 recommendations. Specific personnel should be identified to implement recommendations during the 1978-1979 academic year. Timetables for implementation of the recommendations over the next five years is recommended. Many of the recommendations could aid in student retention and cut attrition. The report should be disseminated and discussed with the President, Vice Presidents, Academic Deans, and Directors before implementation. The committee wishes to meet with the Vice Presidents to discuss the 53 recommendations.

The above premises served as a catalyst for developing a consultation contract for implementing the recommendations. They provided background and justifications for the recommendations in the broader context of societal discrimination. The premises reminded the institution of its responsibilities to act, its previous commitment to educational equity, and how the recommendations could help student retention. They also established the need for budgetary support and timetables for implementation for each recommendation. Finally, they served as the catalyst for the next step, which was further discussion between the consultant, Vice Presidents, and other administrators.

Consultation Phase III:
Problem Identification and Diagnostic Analysis (Activity 3)

The identification of the problem (i.e., racism and sexism) and the diagnostic analysis of the institution's current areas of noncompliance had been accomplished through the Title IX Self Evaluation Report and the committee's final report. The identified consultation problem was how to stimulate a reaction to the report that would promote lasting change. The committee decided to ask for a meeting with the Executive Vice President and vice presidents to insure that the report did not "collect dust" in administrative offices. The Executive Vice President agreed to a meeting, thereby giving the committee an opportunity to discuss the report and move to consultation activities focused on the implementation of the recommendations. The chairperson wrote a memo to each vice president specifying the agenda of the meeting including: (a) reactions to the committee's report, (b) next steps toward implementing the recommendations, and (c) whether the recommendations would receive budgetary support.

Consultation Phases IV and V:
Setting Goals, Taking Action, and Cycling Feedback (Activities 4-18)

The goals of the consultation were communicated through the cover letter accompanying the final report. As discussed above they were: (a) to obtain budgetary support for implementing the recommendations, (b) to assign personnel to each recommendation and a timetable for implementation, (c) to disseminate and discuss the report with major administrators, (d) to establish a meeting between the committee and the vice presidents to discuss the report. They are detailed below.

A number of meetings occurred during this phase of the consultation, which Table 6.1 enumerates. The critical incidents included : (1) first meeting with vice presidents, (2) memo on committee's prioritizing of recommendations, (3) second meeting with vice presidents, (4) the consultant's individual meetings with the vice presidents, (5) memo establishing recommendations that could be implemented without cost; (6) meeting with campus groups and individuals on the status of the recommendations, (7) media exposure of the recommendations, (8) generating a chronological history of the consultation and disseminating it to the media and Executive Vice President, and (9) public exposure of recommendations and acceptance. Each of these is described below:

1. First Meeting With Vice Presidents (Activity 4). The agenda for this meeting was set by the consultant and included: (a) obtaining reactions to the 53 recommendations from the vice presidents, (b) discussing the next steps toward assignment of tasks and implementation, and (c) ascertaining whether the 53 recommendations were budgetary priorities for the university (Committee memo, October 18, 1978). The meeting was low key and cordial. However, the vice presidents indicated that the report was so comprehensive that they wanted the committee to prioritize the recommendations into those needing immediate, versus long-term, attention and immediate, versus long-term, budget priority. The consultant polled the disbanded committee using a questionnaire and formulated the ranks of the 53 recommendations in each area of the report.

2. Prioritizing Recommendations (Activities 5-8). The consultant reported the committee's ranking through a memo that was sent to the Executive Vice President and the other vice presidents. The essence of this memo is best described in the excerpts of the text of the memo:

> The committee hopes that the priorities listed in this memo and the entire report will be given your serious consideration and thought. The committee will be interested in your budgetary decisions and hopefully during our January 16, 1979 meeting, we can discuss how the budget is taking form in terms of our suggestions.
>
> As was mentioned at our November 20 meeting, these recommendations represent a direct attempt to more fully humanize the living and learning environment of the University. Additionally, the recommendations have the potential to improve our academic instruction as well as cut attrition and facilitate retention of students. Lastly, the recommendations have the potential to reduce the direct and indirect discrimination that have been subtly, but fully integrated into our University's institutional structures. Although there was a time when these issues were threatening to individuals and institutions (late 1960s), we believe our society has matured to the point where we can sensitively and proactively attack the social-political problems of discrimination without violence, disruption, or insult. We hope that you share our sentiments about the importance of these issues and that the University will demonstrate through a budget its commitment to reducing sexism and racism on this campus. The commitments will again demonstrate areas where the University is a national leader as an institution that simultaneously values racial, sexual, and cultural pluralism and academic vigor and excellence.

3. Second Meeting With Vice Presidents (Activity 9). The meeting was focused on whether there would be a budget for the ranked recommendations. The exchanges were honest, intense, and periodically confrontational between the consultant and one of the vice presidents. The consultant was told by one vice president that he should be more involved with his teaching and research at that point in his career. The Executive Vice President and the Vice President for Student Affairs provided balance, but it was clear that there would be no budget for the recommendations because of retrenchment issues and limited budget from the legislature. The meeting ended without resolution and the future of the recommendations remained unclear. The consultation had reached an impasse and the first major resistance to change had occurred.

4. Individual Meetings With Vice Presidents (Activity 10). After the second meeting, the consultant decided that the next step was to interview each vice president personally to determine their individual views of the recommendations. Appointments were made after consulting with the Vice President for Student Affairs to insure that this might be a useful next step. The interview consisted of asking each vice president what their level of commitment was to the recommendations and what next steps should occur. The results of these interviews indicated support for the recommendations but a reluctance to specify the next immediate steps. In at least one case it was recommended that the committee had completed their job and that the consultant should "back off." The consultant's final meeting was with the Executive Vice President. The topics discussed emphasized the committee process and what the next steps might be, given the denial of a budget to implement the recommendations. During that meeting, the consultant suggested that some of the recommendations could be implemented without any cost. The Executive Vice President indicated that he would like to consider, as the next step, a list of recommendations that would not cost.

5. Memorandum on Recommendations That Would Not Cost (Activity 11). The consultant wrote a memo that listed 15 recommendations that could be implemented without great cost. The memo also listed targeted populations for each recommendation and the offices and personnel that could be involved in the final implementation. The most confrontational aspect of the memo was its final paragraph. The challenge to the Executive Vice President was communicated through the following statement:

> The success of implementing these recommendations depends on the support of the Administration. Some reallocation of faculty and staff time and other resources may be necessary. Although some of the recommendations may be initially unpopular with some faculty and staff, I do believe that a strong positive case can be built for each recommendation. All of the recommendations are directed at: (1) improving our institutional operations; (2) retaining and attracting new students; (3) reviewing and solidifying our commitments to educational equity for all races and both sexes. In short, these recommendations, with some careful and sensitive planning, can begin the on-going process of eliminating both personal and institutional forms of racism and sexism at the University. Please let me know what the next steps are with these recommendations. I would be available to meet with you and

the other Vice Presidents to discuss the recommendations and how we might move to constructive action. (Memorandum, April 30, 1979)

6. *Meetings With Campus Groups and Individuals on Status of the Recommendations (Activities 12, 13).* The consultant was invited to meet with different groups and individuals to discuss the status of the recommendations. He presented the facts of the consultation process and communicated the general recommendation areas. He also indicated that the recommendations were the responsibility of the university administration to make public and implement.

7. *Media Exposure of Recommendations (Activities 14, 15, 16).* This represented the exposure of the committee, the recommendations, and the consultation process to the University and the city communities. The American Association of University Professors (AAUP) approved a motion to seek release of the entire committee report. The administration had resisted releasing the report for a number of months. Subsequently, it was released to AAUP by the Executive Vice President and two newspaper reports appeared about the committee's work. The president of AAUP was quoted in the city newspaper as saying:

We will look at the recommendations of the task force (that made the 53 recommendations) and see why there was a delay in publishing the report as well as in implementing the regulations, said the president, explaining that the task force, which began meeting in October 1977 had submitted its original report to the Executive Vice President about a year ago.

In September, 1979 the Senate Committee reviewed the committee report. The campus newspaper carried two stories indicating that the Senate was delaying judgment on the 15 recommendations, "to eliminate both personal and institutional racism and sexism at the University." The report was severely criticized by some, supported by others. For instance, three faculty members on the Senate were quoted in the campus newspaper saying:

I find this a very muddled report. It's wretchedly written. It is very provocative. It's a very unfortunate document.

Many of the recommendations should be the responsibility of Affirmative Action.

I dislike seeing the proliferation of committees when we have developed
an Affirmative Action Office.

Ethically, we must look at these recommendations, she said. Some of them
are unmanageable. Some of them are very good. The need to recruit minorities and women for certain fields is obvious.

We need to find out if the recommendations were based on data.

The 15 recommendations were printed for exposure to the campus community in the same articles. The consultant was given an opportunity to
respond to the criticism. Excerpts from the consultant's responses in the
newspaper included:

The report rests with the administration. I have strong confidence that the
administration will act in a responsible way, as they have in the past, on
moving toward a constant assessment in the monitoring of how our institutional structures have the potential to discriminate against people.

I was not surprised by some of the negative reactions. I heard the
objections to the report and I expected that there would be objections to a
report of this kind.

I believe that there is a need for the University community to discuss the
recommendations. It is important to the Committee that the recommendations are received to be discussed and debated by the University community.
The report's goal was to provide recommendations and have them discussed
by the students and faculty.

These responses by the consultant in the media were important to the
continual success of the consultation. Critical discussions with the news
reporters who wrote the stories were found to be essential to insure constructive coverage of the events. The consultant discussed the sensitivity
of the issues and asked for "reporter care" in preparing stories that would
increase the likelihood of constructive change.

8. Chronological History of Consultation Disseminated (Activity 17).
The consultant began to receive numerous inquiries about the status of
the recommendations. Subsequently, the consultant generated a history of
the committee process during the consultation. The three-page history
documented 27 events from October, 1977 to June, 1979. The history
showed how the entire process had developed and who was responsible
for the next steps. The history was then turned over to a news reporter and
sent to the Executive Vice President's office. Dissemination of the history
of the committee and the report established the chain of events and

revealed publicly who was responsible for the final implementation of the recommendations. This dissemination of the history served as a catalyst for the final implementation of the recommendations.

9. Public Exposure of Recommendations and Acceptance (Activity 18). On December 7, 1979, the Executive Vice President released to the president, vice presidents, and the newspapers his decision to implement a majority of the recommendations. The newspaper excerpts best describe the institutional dynamics, including the Executive Vice President's comments, that:

> It is clear that each of us within the University community has an individual responsibility to counteract any persisting instances of sex and race role stereotyping and that we as administrators have a particular responsibility in this area.
>
> Several University offices will be involved in putting them (recommendations) into effect, including the Office of Student Affairs, counselors, residence hall staff, the Offices in the Graduate School, and the Offices of Academic Affairs.

The reporter asked, "According to one of the committee members, administrators might be reluctant to release the report in its entirety because it recorded, probably the first time that the University itself went on record as having problems with discrimination."

> "No I don't think that's accurate," the Executive Vice President explained when asked if that was the reason. "We've acknowledged a number of times that we have a problem in that area. We have trouble recruiting and keeping minorities. There are problems with racism throughout society," he said, adding this university "is no exception."

The consultant was asked for comments about the University decision to implement a majority of the recommendations. The newspaper quotes included:

> Despite the decreased number of recommendations accepted, the Chairperson of the committee said he was encouraged with the University's response. Although not all of the recommendations were accepted, I believe that additional and alternative avenues for change have been suggested by the administration's report. It is a positive first step toward implementation, and

it is also encouraging to know that progress has been made between the time the report was written (completed in May, 1978) and today, he said. But despite the changes within the University, the Chairperson said it was the outcome of these efforts that needs to be monitored and assessed. The University cannot determine whether its procedures to eradicate racism and sexism have been successful, he said, unless the results are studied.

Consultation Phase VI: Contract Completion—Continuity, Support, and Termination (Activities 19-23)

A number of activities finalized the consultation process, including the follow-up evaluations. In July, 1980, the consultant provided the administration with the name of an outside consultant who could provide assistance on how to recruit and retain minority faculty and staff more effectively (Recommendation 12). Additionally, two follow-up evaluations were initiated to assess the effects of the consultation over time. Results from these evaluations are reported in a later section.

Consultation Evaluations

Method of Evaluation. The evaluation of the consultation was completed through various methods over a three-year period. The effects of the consultation were evaluated by the status of the recommendations, a follow-up questionnaire, and an interview with the primary consultee (Executive Vice President). These measures of the outcomes and effectiveness are described below.

Status of Recommendations Proposed. The effectiveness of the consultation was assessed through examining how many of the Committee's recommendations were accepted by the University administration.

Follow-Up Questionnaire. A questionnaire was sent to 48 campus administrators to identify the status of the recommendations 19 months following their acceptance. This questionnaire provided an external and delayed evaluation of consultation outcomes.

Interview. A one-hour, audio-taped, personal interview was conducted with the primary consultee (Executive Vice President) 31 months following the acceptance of the recommendations and one year after the end of the consultation.

Results

Status of the Committee's Recommendations. Eleven of 15 (73%) of the committee recommendations to reduce sex and race role stereotypes on campus were implemented. Recommendations that are starred in Table 6.2 indicate those that were accepted, assigned, completed, partially endorsed, or rejected. Five of the recommendations (1-4, and 13) were accepted and assigned to university administrators. Two recommendations (6 and 11) had already been implemented during the process of consultation. Three recommendations (5, 14, and 15) were accepted in principle but the approaches to implementing them were altered. Three recommendations (7, 8, and 10) were rejected on the grounds that the university administration either could not effectively mandate them or that individual faculty and staff were collectively responsible for implementation. Recommendation 12 was not acted on but was given extensive consideration.

Follow-Up Questionnaire Data of Committee Action—19 Months Later. An assessment of the effects of the recommendations on the university environment was made through a follow-up questionnaire sent to 48 administrators in academic affairs, student affairs, and the graduate school. Four questions were asked of all administrators including: (1) Describe your knowledge about the Committee's activities and recommendations to reduce sex and race role stereotypes; (2) Did any of the recommendations impact your approach to your job and did the person you report to initiate, support, or discuss any of the recommendations with you? (3) Have any of the recommendations resulted in outcomes that can be identified (programs implemented, policy changes, further committees to study the problems)? (4) What was your professional reaction to the recommendations and the work of the committee? Fifty-two percent of the follow-up questionnaires were returned. Responses to each question are summarized below.

The follow-up responses indicated that little information was known about the committee and its recommendations. Half of the respondents indicated that the committee's work had affected their approach to their

TABLE 6.2 Recommendations to Reduce Racism and Sexism That Were Accepted, Assigned, Endorsed, or Rejected

Fifteen Recommendations to Reduce Race and Sex Role Stereotyoing at the University

Recommendation 1: To review how each graduate department recruits and admits students. This review would request that departments report their current policies of recruitment/admissions and to articulate what further steps might be taken to effectively resolve underrepresentation of non-whites and women.

Recommendation 2: To operationalize an annual reporting of total number of students by sex, race, and age in our graduate programs. This information would allow the University to understand trends in student enrollment/attrition and to monitor where there is apparent underrepresentation/discrimination.

Recommendation 3: To survey all graduate and undergraduate departments to assess how each department provides remedial or tutorial help for those students who are failing due to deficiencies in reading, writing, study skills, and other necessary skills to be successful at the University.

Recommendation 4: To survey all graduate departments to assess what admissions criteria are used to admit or reject students. This survey would ask each department to state its admission criteria, justify these criteria in terms of academic excellence, and to explain how these criteria are not discriminatory in terms of race, sex, age, creed, handicap, or sexual persuasion.

** Recommendation 5: To review all academic coursework (graduate & undergraduate) to ascertain whether curricular offerings are representative of our culture in terms of races, both sexes, and across all socio-economic levels. This review would indicate the depth and breadth of multicultural education at the University.

* Recommendation 6: To institutionalize an annual census of students obtaining information on student attitudes and experiences, needs and problem areas and other information that would be valuable to faculty and staff in providing quality classroom instruction and support services.

Recommendation 7: To survey undergraduate and graduate departments to ascertain which departments would co-sponsor in-service programs for their faculty related to sex and race stereotypes that may negatively affect the advising and instructional processes. This survey would be used in the Division of Student Affairs.

Recommendation 8: To implement a training program to annually sensitize all journalists that perform or write in the media to the potential negative effects of sex, race, and religious stereotypes that can be communicated in the media.

* Recommendation 9: To implement in-service training program annually for all residence hall staff to sensitize them to the negative effects of sex and race role stereotypes as they might be manifested in residence hall living.

Recommendation 10: To establish in all residence hall staff members' job descriptions, the specific responsibility of implementing one educational program per year related to the negative effects of sex and race role stereotyping.

* Recommendation 11: To institutionalize a career planning course for academic credit to assist students in career and life planning.

TABLE 6.2 Continued

Fifteen Recommendations to Reduce Race and Sex Role Stereotyoing at the University

**** Recommendation 12: To identify and hire an expert consultant(s) to give advice a
guidance on how to more effectively recruit and retain Black (or other non-white) faculty a
staff and the University.

* Recommendation 13: To survey all academic departments using placement tests to place
admit students to any academic department. This survey would document the tests used, t
rationale for their use, and how they are non-discriminatory.

*** Recommendation 14: To legislate through job descriptions of major administrators
Student Affairs that any office providing direct services to students be required to gath
student evaluation research on the impact and helpfulness of these services. One section
the research would assess students' perceptions of how they were treated in terms of sex a
race role stereotypes.

*** Recommendation 15: To have the Executive Vice President appoint a central steeri
committee to implement the above recommendations and the 53 recommendations specifi
by the Campus Committee to Reduce Sex and Race Role Stereotypes. This steering committ
would decide what next steps are needed, a timetable for implementation, and a means
monitor progress. The Chairperson of this committee should be a major administrator at t
University.

NOTES: * Recommendation accepted and assigned to university administrator.
** Recommendation was implemented during the process of consultation.
*** Recommendation accepted in principle but approach to implementing the recommendation was altere
**** Recommendation not acted on but would be given further consideration.
† Recommendations rejected on grounds that university administration cannot effectively mandate the
or individual faculty and staff are collectively responsible for implementation.

jobs. The other respondents found no direct linkage between changes i
their jobs and the report. One person reported that graduate division ad
missions policies and the policies of the Admissions and Standard
Committee were reviewed because of the report. Another indicated, '
discussed the report with the Vice President to who [sic] I report and ex
pressed my feeling that our office should cooperate with the Committe
to implement all recommendations directly related to our activities." I
Student Affairs, a high-level administrator said, "The recommendation
did reinforce and direct some of my initial efforts in establishing a pro
gram of services for the Division of Student Affairs." A faculty membe
responsible for supervising the campus newspaper wrote :

> As advisor for the campus paper we have had our own staff analysis in the
> area of stereotyping. Although I had already added materials and lectures
> on race and sex stereotyping to the course in advanced reporting I teach
> (these students are the paper's reporting staff), I was encouraged to continue

use of such materials by recommendation 8. I initiated the course material but I believe the Dean and I did discuss recommendation 8 and I indicated that any effort to initiate a training program would find that we were making efforts in that area already.

Identified Outcomes. One of the central difficulties in assessing the outcomes of the recommendations is separating their effects from the naturally occurring events in the campus environment. Three respondents stated that identifiable outcomes related to some of the recommendations occurred but they did not attribute these outcomes to the committee or to the committee report. Conversely, a majority of the respondents identified outcomes that related to the recommendations. These reported outcomes are listed below, with the related recommendations from Table 6.2 found in parentheses:

1. A regular study of student needs has been initiated. (6)
2. A system of ascertaining student opinions and attitudes has been established through the Student Opinion Survey Program. (6)
3. Staff training in Student Affairs has included improved human relations training.
4. Student Affairs has established a regular means of evaluating the impact of its services. (14)
5. Career Planning course was institutionalized. (11)
6. Collection of information about race and sex of students enrolled in our graduate programs was initiated. (2)
7. Graduate School asked department chairperson to include a description of their department's recruitment and admission procedures in their reports made to graduate program review. (1 and 4)
8. Journalism professor responsible for supervising the campus newspaper discussed Recommendation 8 with his dean and additional course material on race and sex role stereotyping were added to his journalism course. (8)
9. An Associate Dean indicated sensitivity to grade inflation problems and grade point average for older applicants were a result of the report. Also, provisional admissions and exceptions policies were established for older students with discrimination concerns in mind. (1 and 4)
10. Hiring a consultant to assist with maintaining and recruiting minority faculty and staff was given thorough consideration by the administration. (12)
11. Graduate School has been particularly active in efforts to identify funds for minority graduate students. (1)

12. Recommendations have produced expanded developmental education programs, student surveys, and analysis of graduate admission requirements procedures in various departments. (3, 6, and 1)

13. A dean indicated that the recommendations were used as part of their school and faculty committee activities in regards to role stereotypes. He also indicated that he was unsure of direct effect of the recommendations but that : (a) his recruitment of undergraduate and graduate students had been given more emphasis; (b) his school has joined a consortium of eight schools to recruit graduate students from black colleges. (1)

14. Student Affairs director reported that the job descriptions of all professional staff members make specific reference to gathering student evaluation research on the impact and helpfulness of their services. (14)

15. A Dean reported starting a program to recruit and work with minority high school students in their summer laboratories. (1)

This list shows that 10 of the 15 recommendations listed in Table 6.2 were reported by respondents as perceived outcomes of the report and committee. Recommendations 1, 4, 6, and 9 were identified by more than one respondent.

Professional Reaction to the Recommendations and Committee. Reactions to the committee and its recommendations were generally positive. Respondents indicated that the committee work was helpful and noteworthy. Specific comments included :

> On balance, they (recommendations) represent thoughtful and constructive contribution toward the solution of a persistent problem.

> I believe the report was extremely helpful and has resulted in some positive changes in the institution. In hindsight, I believe a set of fewer and more workable recommendations might have had a greater impact and acceptance in the university community.

> The task to the committee was so broad and its recommendations are so sweeping that it will be several years before specific effects will be noted.

> I believe that it was worthwhile to focus attention on these issues, but the implementation of the recommendations will be a long-time affair unless an office or individual is given responsibility for "bulldogging" the problem.

In my estimation, the University has made progress in these areas in the years since the committee was first appointed. Some of this progress may result directly from the implementation of specific recommendations; in other instances, results may be directly attributable to the work of the committee, since it most certainly has served to sensitize a number of individuals to the fact that problems of stereotyping do exist, that such stereotyping may be subtle, and that efforts to eradicate it may require considerable effort to eradicate over a long period of time.

Follow-Up Interview With
Executive Vice President 31 Months Later

In July, 1982, two and a half years after the acceptance of the recommendations, a personal interview was conducted with the Executive Vice President, who had returned to his faculty position. The interview was designed to acquire the consultee's assessment of the amount of change that had occurred due to the University's acceptance of the majority of the recommendations, as well as of the consultation process itself. The interview was one hour long, and audio tape recorded.

During the interview, the Executive Vice President recalled that he did not think that much conscious racism and sexism existed on the campus in 1977, when he appointed the Campus Committee to Reduce Race and Sex Role Stereotypes. He did believe that there was unconscious discrimination present that needed attention. He called the change process, "consciousness raising through an educational process." The committee had been formed through a recommendation of the Title IX Self Evaluation Committee, but he indicated that the need for change also came from his own personal-professional value system. He indicated that the committee's recommendations had clearly affected the University and had resulted in institutional change. He gave specific examples of campus committees in Student Affairs as well as Academic Affairs that reflected extensions of the committee's recommendations to reduce racism and sexism on campus. Furthermore, he admitted feeling pressure from all sides regarding the recommendations: indifference from some, support and resistance from his Vice Presidents, pressure from AAUP and the Senate Committee. His approach was to deal directly with all these forces without losing the chance for successful implementation. It was a balancing act with the most extensive effort assigned to developing consensus and support among the vice presidents.

We also discussed the restraining forces that made change difficult. The lack of budget was a major inhibitor for constructive change. No possibility existed for monies to implement the original recommendations since "retrenchment" had already hit the university. Second, the difficulty of dealing with political-social issues such as racism and sexism made the recommendations even more sensitive and difficult. Public reaction and opinion about these issues could have been reactionary and extreme given the University's history in the early 1970s. Third, the depth and comprehensiveness of the recommendations caught the vice presidents and the institution "off guard," leading to some defensive behavior. Some of the vice presidents were concerned about a committee making such comprehensive recommendations that directly affected their areas of responsibility. Other vice presidents were concerned about how to fund the recommendations, how they would fit into their own administrative priorities.

The facilitating forces for change were also enumerated by the Executive Vice President. He indicated the following facilitating forces for change: (a) the vice president's values about issues of discrimination being similar to his own, (b) pending law suits against the university that were reminders of the seriousness of the problem, (c) the influence of the Vice President for Student Affairs in providing rationality and a balanced view of the issues, (d) the chairperson's patience and ability to communicate orally and in writing about where the process stood and not pushing too hard for change before change was possible. In conclusion, he indicated that he should have involved the vice presidents earlier in the process. Also, in retrospect, he thought that involving representatives from the Senate Committee and AAUP could have defused some of the negative reactions to the recommendations. He highly recommended that professionals interested in making institutional change should recognize that every institution is different and, therefore, that it is essential to understand thoroughly each of the opinion leaders. He suggested that consultants study the institutional dynamics that comprise decision making, both from direct and subtle sources of influence. His basic consultation message was "Know your institution (client) and how it responds to change, confrontation, and intergroup dynamics."

Using Multiple Roles and Interventions in the Consultation

The internal consultant became deeply involved in the dynamic processes in the institution where he was employed. Over the months, the consultant interacted with many consultees and responded to various re-actions to the institutional change process. The change process was dif-ficult because the consultation goal was to stimulate an institutional and public response to the recommendations. This goal had potential to alter the institution's approach to the issues of discrimination and to encourage a more direct response to the problems of racism and sexism on the campus.

One of the premises of this casebook is that cyclical, collaborative problem solving is best suited for organizational consultation conducted by counseling psychologists and other human service providers. The consultant and consultees "work together through a series of steps to identify the problem, to generate solutions to it, to design a problem so-lution plan for implementation, to evaluate the effectiveness of that plan, and to recycle feedback along the way as appropriate" (see Chapter 1). This implies moving beyond the traditional prescriptive mode of consul-tation where solutions are provided. This kind of organizational consul-tation implies multiple interventions and consultation roles that span the consultation process. In other words, discovering just what needs to be changed in the organizational setting is usually inadequate for promoting lasting change. Conceptualizing what needs to be done to bring about permanent change over time is the challenge. As stated in Chapter 1, organi-zational consultation implies "more systematic, more long-term involve-ment and study, accompanied by planfully executed and graduated change."

In this case study, the preconsultation activities were clearly prescrip-tive (Blake & Mouton, 1983), meaning that recommendations were gen-erated about how to reduce institutional racism and sexism. The entire consultation process was affected by the prescriptive nature of the recom-mendations to reduce institutional racism and sexism (Blake & Mouton, 1983). As Blake and Mouton observed about prescriptive modes of consultation:

> Regardless of how "right," prescription can and often does increase the client's tensions and block effective problem solving. This is particularly so whenever the prescription goes against the grain of the client's history or dramatically shifts interpersonal, social or working relationships. After such a prescription a shift of intervention mode may be necessary so that the client can explore, express, and work through the emotions and tensions it aroused. (1983, p. 574)

This is exactly what happened after the committee report was submit-ted. There was a strong reaction to the report and the university administrators were taken off guard. They felt defensive and were urged to respond to issues that significantly affected their power and control. These dynamics required new roles and functions for the consultant.

Many clinical-consulting roles and skills were used with multiple consultees over an extended period of time. These roles were similar and dissimilar to the consultant's more common roles of therapist and group leader. The roles were similar because therapeutic skills were used to assess, conceptualize, and intervene as the process emerged. The roles were different because the therapeutic environment was not a counseling office but an entire institution. Once the committee prescribed the recommendations, the consultant used a variety of consultative roles to facilitate change in decreasing racism and sexism on campus. The consultant anguished through difficult times as the consultation moved from prescription to a more comprehensive number of roles. He began the human-development and social/political consultation by using carefully worded memos, thoroughly planned individual and group meetings, data to inform, and presentations on campus to inform others about the status of the recommendations. All of these activities were directed at obtaining an acceptable level of institutional response.

The consultant's process illustrates the need for *multiple* roles and interventions in organizational consultation. Because the consultation was complex and extended over years, many different consultation interventions and multiple roles were used. These roles were implemented and based on the consultant's careful assessment of the consultation dynamics. As more comprehensive and confrontive roles were employed, riskier consultation interactions and problems occurred.

Table 6.3 provides a summary of the multiple interventions and roles employed during the consultation. Each consultation intervention is described using Lippitt and Lippitt's (1986) continuum of roles and phases of consultation. As can be observed in Table 6.3, all of the roles were employed during the consultation. The most common roles in this consultation were advocate, joint problem solver, fact finder, information specialist, and identifier of alternatives-linker of resources. More nondirective roles (i.e., objective observer, process counselor) were also used during other critical times.

The consultant's use of multiple roles raises questions on how certain roles were chosen. Frequently, there was much premeditation when choosing any role or function. Sometimes the roles were chosen intuitively. Other times, selection was based on the interpersonal dynamics existing between the consultant and consultee.

TABLE 6.3 Summary of Consultant's Multiple Roles Using Lippitt and Lippitt's Role Descriptions and Phases of Consultation

Consultation Phase(s)	Consultation Activities or Intervention (see Table 6.1 for Descriptions)	Consultant Role(s)
I & II	1. Submitting the Report and Cover Suggesting Dialogue	Fact Finder Objective Observer Advocate
III	3. Arranging Meeting Time With Vice Presidents and Setting Meeting Agenda	Advocate Joint Problem Solving
IV & V	4. First Meeting With Vice Presidents (Setting the agenda)	Advocate Joint Problem Solving Process Counselor
IV & V	6. Polling the Committee About Recommendations priorities	Fact Finder
IV & V	7. Cover Letter Communicating Recommendations Priorities	Advocate
IV & V	9. Second Meeting With Vice Presidents on Budget Request	Advocate Joint Problem Solving Information Specialist
IV & V	10. Individual Interviews With Vice Presidents About Next Steps With the Recommendations. Meeting with Executive Vice President on Consultation Impasse	Objective Observer Fact Finder Process Counselor Joint Problem Solving Advocate
IV & V	11. Memo on Recommendations That Would Not Cost	Advocate Joint Problem Solving Information Specialist Identifier of Alternatives and Linker to Resources
IV & V	12. Meeting With Campus Groups and Individuals on the Status of the Recommendations	Advocate Identifier of Alternatives and Linker to Resources Joint Problem Solving Information Specialist
IV & V	16. Media Releases and Consultations With News Reporters	Advocate Joint Problem Solving, Information Specialist, Trainer Education
IV & V	17. Disseminating Chronological History of Committee's Work to Media	Process Counselor Fact Finder
VI	19. Finding External Consultant	Identifier of Alternatives and Linker to Resources
VI	20-23. Follow-Up Evaluations and Interview With Executive Vice President	Fact Finder Advocate

Furthermore, the many roles available to consultants raise critical questions about *how to choose* roles during a dynamic consultation process. In therapy, many clinicians rely on the differential treatment question in deciding therapeutic process. The differential treatment question for therapists is: What treatment, for which client, with a specific problem, under which situation, will be most effective, with what expected outcomes? This differential treatment question has implications for consultants who view their clinical consultation as more than prescription. While set within a more complex and dynamic environment, an analogous differential treatment question for consultants is: "What consultation roles and interventions will be most effective, to a specific consultee, who has a specific problem, at a specific time, with what expected outcomes, at what level of effectiveness?" Lippitt and Lippitt's multiple roles provide a comprehensive list of roles for consultants to consider. These roles may be useful to consultants in answering this differential treatment question in long-term, organizational consultations.

Consultant Reactions and Reflections

This consultation was the author's first experience intervening with an entire institution as a consultee. It was one of the most stimulating professional experiences of the author's early career. Overall, the consultant knew he was involved in a new, unique process for addressing critical issues that were vital to institutional growth. On a very personal level, the consultant worked through numerous emotional and professional issues during the consultation. As the advocacy consultation became more confrontive and political the following issues emerged for the consultant: (a) risk, vulnerability, and threat; (b) taking and managing power and control; (c) countertransference, resistance, and safety issues.

Implementing this institutional intervention as an untenured assistant professor led the consultant to feel vulnerable to possible negative evaluation of his overall performance at the University. Vulnerable feelings were stimulated by direct confrontation with consultees who felt threatened by the direction of the consultation. Degrees of threat and risk became more common as the advocacy position more fully emerged. The consultant felt increased threat as the interpersonal dynamics became more tense. For example, the following statements were made to the consultant:

Let me give you some friendly advice! (said with less than friendly tone of voice) You should back off now! You have completed your committee work. It is in *your* interest to stop now. We will take it from here!

(Expressed with anger) There will be no budget for the recommendations this year! We won't and can't do it! What you should do is go back to the School of Education and do your research, teaching, and service. That's what you should be about here. You have those issues to work on here and you have finished the committee work.

These kinds of statements were expressed in individual interviews as well as during a large committee meeting. These exchanges and others triggered worries, fears, and modest amounts of paranoia for the consultant. After these statements, I knew how much impact the consultation was having. It gave the consultant insight into the internal struggles occurring behind the scenes. These statements and reactions were sobering events for the consultant. I began to keep even more extensive notes, sought advice from colleagues outside the university, and decided not to "back off."

The threats and dynamics had mobilized my 1960s activism and suspicion about whether you could work through "The System" for positive change. These interactions also stimulated my negative transferences with abusive authority figures. Yet, my perceptions of the dynamics were different from my 1960s positions. I was acting within a professional consultation role with more knowledge, skill, and personal power. Nonetheless, the political slogans of my earlier years were activated in my mind: "If you're not part of the solution, you're part of the problem"; "Don't just do something, stand there"; "No one is free if any one single person is oppressed."

My negative transferences and anger produced fantasies about what to do with the institution's very slow response to the recommendations. These fantasies lacked objectivity and I was aware they could have derailed the whole process. I felt that I was being given the "administrative run around," and began to doubt the sincerity of the University's commitment to implement the recommendations. With my advocate and radical role becoming stronger, I imagined turning the entire story over to the media with much negative commentary. I thought of contacting individuals who had embarrassed the University administration before because of its inaction. I considered forming a new committee and directly putting pressure on the administrators to respond to the recommendations. Any of these actions would have been counterproductive to the consultation goal. Yet, these ideas were churning around in my head and emanated from my powerlessness, feelings of threat, and impatience with the process.

What mediated all of these reactions were the steady, ongoing, communications with the Executive Vice President. He indicated that something would ultimately happen to the recommendations. I also kept my balance by telling myself that I was in a professional role that required restraint and patience. Also, the delays were conceptualized as consultee resistance. As with individual clients, I recognized that resistance happens and it can change. I knew it takes time, sensitivity, and carefully planned interventions to resolve consultation impasses.

I continued to feel threatened about my own personal status and the possible repercussions on my tenure decision. My consultation activities were supported by the Executive Vice President, but they were also anxiety producing. After all, people who catalyze and confront, even when it may be very professionally appropriate to do so, can get punished personally and professionally. I remember communicating these defensive, protective, and vulnerable lines to certain administrators about my future status at the University:

> I hope that my political activity on campus will not affect my promotion and tenure decision. That would be very unfair and messy for the University to deal with. There would be due cause for a lawsuit and AAUP involvement. That would be very unfortunate and make the institution look very bad given the kind of issues we are trying to make gains (i.e., discrimination, racism, sexism).

I developed ways to increase power and control to advocate for the recommendations and for the discriminated groups. Some power came from chairing the committee and my knowledge about institutional racism and sexism. Other sources of power came from my keen knowledge of the institutional dynamics and the personality characteristics of the primary consultees. Other sources of power developed through my trusting and constructive relationship with the Executive Vice President and, at least, cordial relationships with the other Vice Presidents. There was power because my role was ambiguously defined. Power was there to be taken. No one had *officially* told me that I was "out of line, inappropriate, or pulling rank." I would assume this power and assert more active consultative roles that raised tensions and threats to certain consultees. Then, I would become quite passive and uninvolved, letting the Executive Vice

President work with the process. I stayed in touch enough to let him know I was observing the process and waiting patiently for an institutional response.

Learning how to take control and develop power were old lessons that were relearned in a new context. What was different is that the stakes were higher, knowing that I could be personally affected by the consultation dynamics. I remember saying to myself during the really difficult times that, "if I can't assert these values about eliminating racism/sexism on a campus without being punished, I don't belong at a University and don't want to belong." Giving up power and control that have been painfully gained were new lessons that I learned. It was difficult to back down on our request for a budget to implement the recommendations. It was also difficult to stay in control of myself when I was personally or subtly threatened. I developed approaches to handle my reactions to adverse conditions. When publicly threatened, I would not respond directly to the threats, but would immediately shift the discussion to the reality of discrimination at the University. I would also comment that the five lawsuits pending against the University required a more proactive approach than a legal defense. I viewed the threats as manipulations and knew that I could document every step of the consultation if there were ever any punitive action taken against me. The extensive notes and documentation served as a basis to explain the process if anyone questioned my role and motives.

In the end, both consultant and the consultees were key participants in a demanding and difficult endeavor. Each was motivated by values that they shared in providing equal access in education, regardless of race or sex. Commitment to this basic value enabled them to persist in their respective consultation roles.

I could have been more confident and secure with a more developed conceptualization of the consultation phases, roles, and inevitable power dynamics in both human-development and advocacy consultation. It would have been helpful to have a co-consultant to process the events and plan strategies during the consultation impasses. Even with this kind of processing, there still would have been considerable ambiguity about what to do given the many unknowns and hidden agendas. This consultation stretched my tolerance for ambiguity. Often, there really was no clear course of action. There were many times when I sat back and said, "Well, what do I do now?" And frequently, I just followed my intuition. While intuition can be a vital source of guidance, theoretically based and planned interventions are strongly recommended for all consultants who do organizational consultation.

Implications for Training Consultants

This case study provides additional insights into the future training of consultants. Few comprehensive models of training exist in the consultation literature. It is through documented case studies that we learn what consultants actually do, what consultants need to know, and the skills they need to possess. This case study illustrates some salient training issues relevant to courses in consultation, applied practica, and inservice activities.

First, trainers are encouraged to teach multiple theories of consultation in courses. Because different consultations require different kinds of interventions, consultants need to have multiple ways of conceptualizing the phases, events, and feedback loops that occur in consultation. Likewise, consultants need to learn expert assessment and data gathering skills to make constant consultation appraisals. These skills are particularly important when assessing complex institutional dynamics and the usual power-personality clashes that occur. Additionally, trainers should help trainees understand the multiplicity of consultation roles and the specific skills that are associated with each. This knowledge will better enable consultants to match roles and skills with specific interventions.

Specifically, in organizational consultation, trainers should help future consultants understand the power-control-resistance dynamics that usually are manifested. This may involve helping trainees understand the different kinds of power bases, what happens when power is used or abused, and actually how their own power issues operate within a consultation role. In the same way, "resistance to change," as an organizational reality, needs to be understood and explored. Models of resistance reduction from the therapy literature may need to be adapted to situations in consultation. Another important topic in consultation training should be trainee knowledge of their own interpersonal dynamics when consulting. As was observed in this case, the consultee's own personal issues were stirred as the power dynamics became more intense and volatile. Helping trainees understand their countertransferences is critical in training more clinically expert consultants. Knowing yourself, in the context of your role and the specific consultation situation, may be the single most important factor for success.

Consultation as a mechanism to reduce undesirable societal conditions (i.e., sexism and racism) is not for the consultant who is either "faint of heart" or untrained. As can be clearly seen in this case study, the endeavor demanded competence, not only in these areas but in such areas as political maneuvering and persistent facilitation of change (Conyne, 1977). Interventions such as this one are typically time demanding and difficult. Nonetheless, because institutionalized racism and sexism can victimize and traumatize people, these phenomena can be prioritized targets for consultants who are committed to eliminating societal oppression and promoting social justice. When constructive change is documented, it supports the consultant's critical role of changing the racist and sexist institutions that ultimately violate, victimize, and oppress us all.

References

Albee, G. W., & Joffe, J. M. (1977). *The issues: An overview of primary prevention.* Hanover, NH: University of New England.

Auerback, A. (1973). The psychological health of the city today. In J. L. Carleton & U. Mahlendorf (Eds.), *Man for man: A multidisciplinary workshop on affecting man's social and psychological nature through community action* (pp. 270-272). Springfield, IL: Charles C Thomas.

Blake, R. R., & Mouton, J. S. (1983). *Consultation: A handbook for individual and organizational development* (2nd ed.) Reading, MA: Addison-Wesley.

Conoley, J., & Conoley, C. (1982). *School consultation: A guide to practice and training.* Elmsford, NY: Pergamon.

Conyne, R. K. (1975). Environmental assessment: Mapping for counselor action. *Personnel and Guidance Journal, 54*(3), 151-154.

Conyne, R. K. (1977). The campus change advocate. *Journal of College Student Personnel, 18,* 312-316.

Conyne, R. (Chair), Banning, J., Clack, R,. Corazzini, J., Huebner, L., Keating, L., & Wrenn, R. (1978). Summary report of the campus environment as client: Considerations and implications for counseling psychology. *The Counseling Psychologist, 7*(3), 72.

Conyne, R. K., & Clack, R. (1975). The consultation intervention model: Direction for action. *Journal of College Student Personnel, 16,* 413-417.

Hamilton, M. K., & Meade, C. (1979). Consulting on campus. In U. Delworth & G. Hanson (Eds.), *New directions for student services.* San Francisco: Jossey-Bass.

Gallessich, J. (1985). Toward a meta-theory of consultation. In D. Brown & D. Kurpius (Eds.), Consultation [Special issue], *The Counseling Psychologist, 13,* 336-354.

Leonard, M. M. (1977). The counseling psychologist as an organizational consultant. *The Counseling Psychologist, 7*(2), 73-77.

Lippitt, G., & Lippitt, R. (1986). *The consulting process in action* (2nd ed.). La Jolla, CA: University Associates.

Moyers, W. (1971). *Listening to America.* New York: Harper's Magazine Press.

Title IX of the Education Amendments of 1972: Prohibition of Sex Discrimination. (1972). P.L. 92-318, enacted June 23, U.S. Code, Title 20, Sec. 1681.

7

Analysis and Synthesis of the Case Studies: Some Lessons Learned for Future Consultants

ROBERT K. CONYNE

JAMES M. O'NEIL

DAVID A. FRAVEL

STEVEN P. KRAKOFF

LYNN S. RAPIN

DONALD I. WAGNER

JOSEPH E. ZINS

IN this final chapter, we want to draw some lessons for consultation from the detailed case studies that have been presented. Particularly, we address four important issues:

- Barriers faced in consultation
- Consultation strategies that appeared to work
- Implications for consultation training
- Using the consultation cases in training

Consultation Barriers

As we have seen in these cases, each consultant confronted a wide range of challenges and barriers, and we will highlight only a few for illustration purposes. Zins, in his school-based consultation, had to earn trust the hard way due to the negative residual affect resulting from the previous consultant's work. Rapin, in her social service consultation, was continuously pulled by consultees to behave as a "super staff person," the consequences of which would have meant abrogating her external consultant positioning and objectivity. O'Neil and Conyne, in their university consultation, reported the difficulties of consulting around the highly sensitive and politicized issues of racism and sexism, and the multiple and often conflicting agendas held strongly by occupants of different elements, both on and off campus. Wagner and Krakoff, in their health systems consultation, had to cope with a mid-stream change in health care administration and its concomitant pressures upon the ongoing consultation effort. Fravel and O'Neil found that the consulting world never stood still in the turbulent environment of a financial services organization in transition.

A clear lesson that emerges from the cases is that consultation is frequently an "upstream" process, not unlike the route of the salmon trying to leap the waterfalls to the spawning area. It is often tough work, full of rocks, reefs, eddies, predators, surprises, and unknown obstacles. Three central forces to be contended with by many consultants are: (a) consultee resistance, (b) complex circumstances, and (c) professional isolation. Each of these forces is discussed below, followed by some consultant strategies that seem to be helpful in addressing them.

Consultee Resistance. A dominant barrier every consultant faces is resistance (Randolph & Graun, 1988). This dynamic is commonplace because a consultant represents the threat of change in a client system, whether at the individual, group, or organizational level. Change is scary, no matter how much a consultee feels a need for it, or desires it to occur.

Resistance is manifested in a variety of ways, only a few of which we can mention here. Sometimes consultees will provide only partial access to the information, people, or resources necessary for the activity to occur effectively. They may approach consultation ambivalently, participating in activities aimed at change while holding fast to existing practices and attitudes that have contributed to the problem. Occasionally, members of consultee systems may openly challenge the consultation or, perhaps more frequently, silently work to subvert it. All too often, consultation has been mandated from "above" somewhere, so that the consultee naturally approaches the activity with trepidation, mistrust, and denial. Consultees also can hold tenaciously to the position of the consultant as a "problem fixer," where they expect consultation to take place somehow outside their involvement and without their investment.

Complex Circumstances. A second significant consultation barrier is complexity. This condition emerges naturally from the structural nature of the intervention and from the helping context within which consultation must occur. The indirect structure of the consultation process, where the consultant attempts to aid a client system through a consultee, injects an additional layer of activity for the consultant. So what is part of the multiplicative power of the intervention contributes to some palpable difficulties in conducting it. Additionally, consultation is imbued with contextual concerns. Attempts to help consultees become better workers, to handle tasks more effectively, to improve their organizations, and so on, by necessity demand that the consultant consider complex, dynamic and frequently chaotic, and highly unpredictable conditions.

Professional Isolation. A final tall barrier we emphasize is that consultants frequently feel lonely, overpowered, and unsure. They are often looked to as being a kind of "savior," which they can never be (nor, in our opinion, should they ever—for even a moment—consider), so expectations and demands can be unrealistically high. They must work hard with consultees to convert their expectancies into achievable goals while mobilizing consultee efforts productively, even as resistance and complexity swirl around them. Combined with the fact that many consultants work alone, this confluence of forces can serve to vitiate consultant effectiveness. Consultants can allow deeply painful emotions and concerns to ensnare them, especially if they are without support locally and/or perceive their functions are unsupported by their profession. Thus both a personal and professional sense of isolation can develop, with debilitating consequences.

Consultation Strategies That Appeared to Work

Fortunately, the case study material suggests some strategies that other consultants can use to anticipate and to cope with the barriers they will encounter. We will organize these strategies by the categories used above to discuss barriers: Consultee Resistance, Complex Conditions, and Professional Isolation.

Resistance-Reducing Strategies

Several strategies appear to be useful in reducing consultee resistance and in mobilizing productive work. We will highlight three of them in this section: work collaboratively, establish and maintain trust, and know when to use multiple roles.

Work Collaboratively. Avoid the temptation, and the invitation, to define your position as an expert provider or a prescriber of solutions. Create a situation in which your expertise (e.g., in group process or in prevention skills) can interact with the consultee's expertise (e.g., their knowledge of the situation) to produce interdependent efforts to problem-solve and arrive at decisions and actions that both of you can endorse. The successful consultation efforts reported in these cases all took this precept seriously.

Establish and Maintain Trust. Trust is not arrived at one day and then somehow continues of its own free will. Trust is earned every inch of the way, every minute of the consultation. Treating people with respect, involving them, doing what you say you will do, behaving ethically and morally, hearing and responding to painful feelings and issues, sharing yourself appropriately, demonstrating concern, searching for valid information, giving credit where it is due, and clearly defining responsibilities are all a part of this process. The long-term consultations reported in this book enabled these and other aspects of trust-building to be identified, and they underscored the critical nature of trust maintenance throughout the life of a consultation.

Know When to Employ Different Roles. These long-term cases suggest that multiple roles are necessary in consultation. While all consultants approached their work within the overarching ideological human-development system, each consultant used roles drawn from the other systems to accomplish goals. O'Neil and Conyne reported use of advocacy to catalyze consultee consideration of institutional racism and sexism; Wagner and Krakoff drew from the expert information role in providing training in health promotion strategies; Rapin did the same in teaching program development and evaluation methods to social service staff; Zins used his expertise in testing and assessment to provide service evaluations to school personnel; Fravel and O'Neil developed training models that were employed with financial service staff, and so on. Different modes of working are necessary at various points in a human-development consultation. Resistance can be reduced by selecting an appropriate role within a collaborative, problem-solving context. As Schein (1989) has indicated with regard to process consultation, one should always start in the process consultation mode but a consultant should not withhold his or her expertise if it is really needed.

Complexity-Reducing Strategies

These long-term organizational consultations were situated within complex and dynamic environments. Sometimes these settings were experienced by staff and consultants alike as chaotic. All consultation brings with it aspects of unpredictability and uncertainty. As O'Neil and Conyne observed in their case study on institutional racism and sexism, consultation is not for the faint of heart. We will emphasize three consultation strategies that emerge from the cases and that seem to hold potential for other consultants in managing complexity. Although in reality these three strategies inexorably interact, for the sake of discussion only, we treat them separately. These strategies are: know consultation, know the consultee system, and know yourself.

Know Consultation. Various competing models or ideas of consultation have been developed. As with counseling, teaching, or other modes of helping, it is critical that the consultant understands and effectively incorporates a working model of consultation. Sometimes we think it may be even more important for a consultant to be guided by a model because of the particular nuances and demands inherent within consultation and the diverse settings where it can be employed. Having a conceptual template to follow, such as that provided in the human-development system, frees consultants to be more open to their experience and enables them to proceed with necessary confidence.

Know the Consultee System. It is essential for consultants to understand the consultee system, of whatever size and however many levels. Knowing the system demands answers to a number of questions, including:

- What is the nature of the problem?
- Who experiences the problem?
- What subsystems are involved?
- Who is requesting consultation?
- How is consultation understood?
- What are the resources available?
- What works and what does not?
- What will be the specific aspects of the consultation contract?
- Who will do what, by when, with what resources?
- How will results be determined?
- Where are the supports for potential change?
- Where are the resistances to such change?
- What has been tried in the past?
- What is the history of the consultee system?

Assessing the consultee system is absolutely critical to the success of any consultation effort. Considerable time and effort should generally be expended on this step. Information yielded can provide the necessary foundation to guide subsequent consultation phases.

Know Yourself. Consultation theory, technique, and skills are all important in consultation. However, we believe that there is no substitute for consultants who are self-aware and who can apply their natural strengths productively. As the cases have shown amply, the consultants needed to exercise patience, persistence, flexibility, determination, risk-taking, sensitivity, expertise, trust, and more. Perhaps it is the dynamism and unpredictability inherent in consultation contexts that demand consultants to be especially highly adaptive and flexible, in addition to other characteristics associated classically with helping functions. So consultants need to be well-grounded in theory, knowledge, and skills *and* they need to be ready for nearly anything.

The casebook authors shared an interesting experience while presenting a symposium on these cases at the 1990 meeting of the American Psychological Association. Right in the middle of the symposium the Convention Hall's emergency siren sounded, an emergency light in the symposium room began flashing, and an official voice coming through the Hall's loudspeaker demanded that all in attendance evacuate the building immediately and in an orderly fashion due to an emergency somewhere in the building. Thousands of convention attendees followed suit, including us, not knowing what accounted for the emergency (it turned out to be a false alarm), but realizing that each of their programs was suddenly ended! We conferred on the way out of the building and decided to continue our symposium on the street. A few stout-hearted members of our audience continued with us as we presented our cases on the sidewalk, amidst sirens, interruptions, hot sun, and considerable confusion. It occurred to all of us that this event, and our response to it, reflected much of what consultants experience—the unpredictable will happen, the issue is how to anticipate and respond when it does.

In addition to maintaining qualities of adaptiveness in coping with complexity, consultants can improve their capacity to sort through the maze of events by implementing reflective techniques. For instance, O'Neil and Conyne attended to the use of memos and personal notes throughout their consultation, and Zins discussed the importance of self-monitoring strategies in his work. It is sometimes difficult in consultation to separate the "forest from the trees," because so much occurs. Intentionally and consistently engaging in self-reflective practices can enable consultants to process events and their role in them more effectively. This form of action research or action science (Argyris, Putnam, & Smith, 1987) is associated with improved practice and research.

Isolation-Reducing Strategies

We have never heard such expressions of isolation from colleagues as we have from fellow consultants. At the same time, consultants seem to experience exhilaration more frequently than others. Strategies for reducing isolation need to be developed, and we offer three suggestions based on the cases in this book: develop a peer support network, engage in some variety of activities, and increase professional support.

Develop a Peer Support Network. Danger—Consultants should not be independent agents! Perhaps this should become a warning label affixed to all graduates of training programs. That is to say, it is fine for consultants to work alone, if they choose and are able, but they should be encouraged to find a functional way to connect with peers for purposes of learning and support. Such networks should be formed and made accessible to consultants so that feelings of isolation are prevented or at least reduced.

Engage in Some Variety of Activities. The consultants in this casebook all performed other activities in addition to consultation. They were professors, private practice psychologists, administrators, trainers, and so on. This diversity of functions may serve to counterbalance the difficult demands associated with the consultation enterprise.

Increase Professional Support. Counseling Psychology mirrors many helping professions in that consultation occupies a lower rung in the training and delivery hierarchy, with some exceptions. Those professionals who perform consultation without benefiting from professional support (or organizational support from their own employing agency) can feel diminished and unacknowledged. Advocating for change within professional circles may be one necessary strategy for bringing about the kind of support that is needed.

Implications for Consultation Training

Students must be taught more than the technical competencies of consultation, although they are an essential part (Brown, 1985). Among other accomplishments, trainees must grasp the intersection of knowledge, skills, and judgment; how consultation processes develop; group and organizational dynamics; interpersonal relations; how to assess and conceptualize consultation settings; and how to apply professional judgment— including professional ethics—to ongoing consultation experience.

In fact, the application of professional judgment, which is implied but not fully explicated within all consultation competencies, seems especially important for consultants to master. The particular barriers consultants have to face in their work, such as high complexity and isolation, pose significant and ambiguous challenges. Professional judgment includes the effective incorporation of professional ethics (American Psychological Association, 1981; American Psychological Association, 1991) to consultation practice and issues, a matter sorely in need of attention not only in training but by the professions themselves (Crego, 1985; Lowman, 1985; Robinson & Gross, 1985). Trainees must become adept as reflecting, ethical practitioners in order to maintain their effectiveness. Processing, analyzing, reviewing, attributing meaning, evaluating, researching, inquiring, weighing alternatives—these reflection behaviors will need to be naturally and continually embedded within consultation training. In addition, students should be exposed specifically to ethical situations that can occur in consultation in order to increase their competence as ethical consultants.

In reviewing all the consultation cases reported in this book, we were very impressed with the importance of consultants being able to conceptualize the consultee system and the resulting attention they gave not only to the more familiar human-relations factors but also to broader systemic ones. Consultants in training not only need to learn models (or, maybe, one model in depth) of consultation, but also to learn how to understand consultation settings, such as work groups and organizations.

To this end, an ecological, systems orientation offers unique advantages over others. Consultants need to learn how to analyze a setting, such as a school, a corporation, or a mental health center, according to its constituent elements: context, structure, goals, work procedures, personnel, human processes, leadership, and technologies (Pascale & Athos, 1981; Weisbord, 1978). Then, they need to learn how to understand the ways in which those elements interact, because interdependence, not independence, characterizes settings (Morgan, 1986).

A closely related aspect of understanding and applying an ecological, systems perspective to consultation is the importance of assessing the culture of a setting (Schein, 1985, 1990). A working comprehension is needed of the basic assumptions, values, and artifacts that run throughout the setting. Such an understanding of organizational culture is important for any successful organizational consultation. Cultural assessment is absolutely fundamental to what Porras and Silvers (1991) have termed "organizational transformation," a process that is directed at creating a new vision for the organization. Among other necessities, it takes an ample amount of time, an ecological-systemic approach, and the use of qualitative research methods for consultants to learn about the culture of a setting.

In order to apply the ecological, systems conceptual approach in their work, future consultants will need excellent assessment competencies, the capacity to establish contracts and work effectively with consultees, superb human process and group facilitation skills, and well-developed technical skills. The cases in the book are replete with excellent examples of how the consultants were able to employ advocacy and technical expert roles and skills, when necessary—as trainers, program developers, lobbyists, informational experts, and evaluators—to assist consultees and their systems to advance in desired directions.

A final training concept we wish to emphasize is empowerment, or the capacity of consultants to help consultees to transform their work or their work settings. Empowerment has been implied throughout the continuing discussion in this book of collaborative problem solving and the human-development system of consultation. We think that empowerment represents a desirable overarching value system for consultation that would clarify and organize the specific processes of a consultation training program.

In our view, consultation training should be set securely within a clear value system so that didactic, experiential, and supervised field practice can occur with coherence. An empowerment value system, coupled with an ecological, systems perspective, provides a basic framework capable of guiding the evolution of training that will be needed by future consultants.

Using the Casebook in Consultation Training and Practice

We developed the descriptions of these consultation cases to be useful in narrowing the discrepancy between training and practice in consultation. It is our fervent hope that this material will be used by practitioners and within training programs to assist in this mission and, more importantly, to advance the effectiveness of consultation delivery. Therefore, considering how to use the case material in courses and training experiences becomes necessary.

The cases can be used in consultation training as part of assigned readings and to further class discussions. Students can study the cases with a specific focus on the consultation process, dynamics, and complex events that are described. Instructors could assign homework centering specifically on a case or parts of a case and the cases could be compared and contrasted. For example, was Rapin's case any different than Zins's in terms of consultation issues, plan, and implementation? Were power, control, and consultation competence dealt with differentially in the cases? There are a host of other questions that trainees could answer to make the cases relevant and meaningful training experiences.

Students could be asked to describe, in their own words, what the consultation process was like in each case. To personalize the cases, students could be asked to indicate how they would have handled certain aspects of the consultations. Furthermore, analysis of the tension points in each case can help trainees identify trigger events that affected the entire consultation. Having students identify the restraining and facilitating forces, using a force field analysis (see Fravel and O'Neil, Chapter 4 this volume) can help learners internalize the "nitty gritty" of these cases, beyond a mere reading of the chapters. Just as a consultant has to deal with ambiguity and complexity, students can be asked to synthesize both the process and internal dynamics of the cases. Similar to a practicing consultant, students should be given a chance to explore beyond the overt consultation dynamics to the core of the problem and the deeper organization dynamics. The cases serve as training stimuli, encouraging students to think from a systems perspective and to embrace the complexity of organizational (and other forms of) consultation.

As is apparent, the cases are complex. A full analysis of each consultation by students can provide an approach to assessing consultant behavior along a variety of dimensions, including the five phases of consultation identified by Lippitt and Lippitt (1986). This kind of analysis permits a vivid illustration of how consultants move through the cyclical, collaborative, problem-solving process described in Chapter 1. Likewise, analysis of the roles employed at different phases (for example, see Chapters 4 and 6) can fully communicate how role selection and flexibility are imperative during the consultation process.

A summary of the consultant's personal reflections can underscore the real life personal processes that consultants experience. Personalizing consultation can assist students to realize how their own personal-psychological issues can be activated during the consultation process. The countertransference issues faced by consultants need to be emphasized in consultation supervision just as they are in counseling practica and internships. There are as many approaches to using the casebook in classes and training workshops as there are creative ideas of the trainer.

Finally, however the book is used in training, it is our hope that its case material will help reduce any ambivalence about consultation being an important intervention that can be used to empower client systems and consultees. The challenge is for greater numbers of programs to provide necessary and sufficient consultation training, allowing trainees to develop the resources necessary for them to use the intervention effectively. Only then can the gap be closed between consultation practice and training.

References

American Psychological Association. (1981). *Ethical principles of psychologists*. Washington, DC: Author.

American Psychological Association. (1991). Draft of APA Ethics Code published. *Monitor, 22*(6), 31-35.

Argyris, C., Putnam, R., & Smith, D. (1987). *Action science*. San Francisco: Jossey-Bass.

Brown, D. (1985). The preservice training and supervision of consultants. In D. Brown & D. Kurpius (Eds.), Consultation [Special issue], *The Counseling Psychologist, 13*(3), 410-425.

Crego, C. (1985). Ethics: The need for improved consultation training. In D. Brown & D. Kurpius (Eds.), Consultation [Special issue], *The Counseling Psychologist, 13*, 473-476.

Lowman, R. (1985). Ethical practice of psychological consultation. In D. Brown & D. Kurpius (Eds.), Consultation [Special issue], *The Counseling Psychologist, 13*, 466-472.

Morgan, G. (1986). *Images of organization*. Newbury Park, CA: Sage.

Pascale, R., & Athos, A. (1981). *The art of Japanese management: Applications for American executives*. New York: Warner.

Porras, J., & Silvers, R. (1991). Organizational development and transformation. *Annual Review of Psychology, 42*, 51-78.

Randolph, D., & Graun, K. (1988). Resistance to consultation: A synthesis for counselor-consultants. *Journal of Counseling and Development, 67*, 182-184.

Robinson, S., & Gross, D. (1985). Ethics of consultation: The Canterville ghost. In D. Brown & D. Kurpius (Eds.), Consultation [Special issue], *The Counseling Psychologist, 13*(3), 444-465.

Schein, E. (1985). *Organizational culture and leadership*. San Francisco: Jossey-Bass.

Schein, E. (1989). Process consultation as a general model of helping. *Bulletin: Consulting Psychology, 41*, 3-15.

Schein, E. (1990). Organizational culture. *American Psychologist, 45*, 109-119.

Weisbord, M. (1978). *Organizational diagnosis*. La Jolla, CA: University Associates.

Index

About the Contributors

Robert K. Conyne is a graduate of Syracuse University, and received his Master's and Doctorate in Counseling from Purdue University. He completed a Postdoctoral Internship in Counseling Psychology from the University of California-Berkeley. He was employed for nine years at Illinois State University as a Counseling Center psychologist and as a Professor of Counselor Education. Following a year as Visiting Scholar in Community Psychology and the Counseling Services at the University of Michigan, he joined the University of Cincinnati, where he has served as Associate Vice Provost in Student Affairs and Professor of Counseling, and for the past five years as Head of the School Psychology and Counseling Department.

He was Editor of the *Journal for Specialists in Group Work* for six years. He has written and presented more than 125 scholarly works, several book chapters, and four books in the areas of consultation, group work, and primary prevention—areas in which he consults to universities, schools, and human services.

He is a Fellow of the Division of Counseling Psychology, and the Division of Consulting Psychology of the American Psychological Association, the American Psychological Society, and the Association for Specialists in Group Work of the American Association for Counseling and Development now named the American Counseling Association.

David A. Fravel is a graduate of the College of the Holy Cross. He has more than 21 years of business experience working at the executive level in the financial services industry. He is a Chartered Life Underwriter, a Fellow of the Life Office Management Institute, and an Associate Fellow in the Academy of Life Underwriting. He has also pursued graduate level courses in counseling psychology. He served as an internal process consultant to the organization covered in the consultation chapter co-written with O'Neil. He maintains a strong professional interest in consultation as a helping service to organizations undergoing change, particularly organizations undergoing change as a result of the implementation of new technologies.

Steven P. Krakoff has a master's degree in business administration from The Ohio State University and a bachelor's degree in urban planning from the University of Cincinnati. He is currently a principal with Krakoff Strategic Concepts, an international marketing and consulting firm based in Columbus, OH. Previously he was Assistant Vice-President of Planning and Marketing with a midwestern multihospital system, and also held marketing positions with a Fortune 500 manufacturer of consumer and health care products.

His current professional interests include social marketing and international business competitiveness. He is presently advising U.S. and Brazilian health care organizations on social marketing issues. Also, as part of Brazil's transition to a more open economy, his company is helping to train current and future Brazilian business leaders on how to enhance that country's global business competitiveness. From 1987-1989, he was a Fellow in International Development with the W. K. Kellogg Foundation and the National Association of Partners of the Americas.

James M. O'Neil, Ph.D, is Professor of Family Studies and Educational Psychology at the University of Connecticut, Storrs. From 1982 to 1990 he was Professor of Counseling Psychology in the Department of Educational Psychology at the University of Connecticut. A licensed psychologist in private practice, he also provides counseling, psychotherapy, and consultation services in South Windsor, CT, and the greater

Hartford area. In 1975, he received his Ph.D. from the University of Maryland's Counseling and Personnel Services Department.

At a national level, he has been elected or appointed to numerous editorial boards and committees. He was appointed to the editorial board of the *Journal of Counseling Psychology* from 1980-1985 and has served on the *Psychology of Women Quarterly* editorial board from 1986 to the present. He was elected to Fellow status in the American Psychological Association (Division 35—Psychology of Women) in 1991. He currently serves on the steering committee of the newly formed Society for the Psychological Study of Men and Masculinity of the American Psychological Association.

In 1990, he was awarded the Thomas M. Magoon Distinguished Alumni Award by University of Maryland's Counseling and Personnel Services Department. In 1991, he was awarded a Fulbright Teaching Scholarship by the Council for International Exchange of Scholars, to lecture in the Soviet Union. He lectured at the Moscow State Pedagogical University from February through April, 1992, on the topics of psychological counseling and career development.

Lynn S. Rapin, Ph.D., is a Cincinnati-based Counseling Psychologist who devotes her time to consultative and psychotherapeutic interventions. In consulting with health, human service and business organizations, she has employed a broad range of consultation strategies with executive, department, and line-staff organization members. She received her Ph.D. from the University of Illinois, has served on the faculty of Illinois State University, and has been an Adjunct Associate Professor in the University of Cincinnati Department of School Psychology and Counseling since 1981. She has served on the Editorial Board of the *Journal for Specialists in Group Work,* and has been on the faculty of the University of Cincinnati College of Business Executive Program. She has presented or published more than 40 papers in the areas of consultation, program development, and group work. She is currently co-authoring a book on collaborative problem solving in organizations.

Donald I. Wagner, H.S.D., received his doctorate from Indiana University. He has served as a member of the faculty of the University of Cincinnati since 1974, and is currently Professor of Family Medicine and Health Promotion. He serves as Director of the Office of Health Promotion and Disease Prevention, and is a former Kellogg/Partners of the Americas Fellow in International Development. He was named the Senior Adviser for Health Promotion and Disease Prevention to the Brazilian

Ministry of Health in 1990. Also, he has served as a consultant on health promotion for the World Bank. He has a variety of publications in the area of health promotion and health education.

Joseph E. Zins, Ph.D., is a Professor in the Department of Early Childhood and Special Education at the University of Cincinnati, and has been a psychological consultant with the Beechwood (KY) Independent Schools for nine years. He has nearly 90 publications on consultation and prevention, and is co-editor of the forthcoming text, *The Handbook of Consultation Services for Children.* Professor Zins serves as a section editor of the *Journal of Educational and Psychological Consultation* and is a Fellow of the American Psychological Association. He is currently investigating procedures directed toward enhancing the consultation process and facilitating peer collaboration.